OF CANNIBALS AND KINGS

OF CANNIBALS AND KINGS

Primal Anthropology in the Americas

Neil L. Whitehead

The Pennsylvania State University Press
University Park, Pennsylvania

Library of Congress Cataloging-in-Publication Data
Whitehead, Neil L.
Of cannibals and kings : primal anthropology in the
Americas / Neil L. Whitehead.
     p.   cm.—(Latin American originals ; v. 7)
Includes bibliographical references and index.
Summary: "Translations of the earliest accounts,
from the fifteenth and sixteenth centuries, of the
native peoples of the Americas, including Columbus's descriptions of his first voyage. Documents the
emergence of a primal anthropology and how Spanish
ethnological classifications were integral to colonial
discovery, occupation, and conquest"—Provided by
publisher.
ISBN 978-0-271-03799-8 (pbk. : alk. paper)
1. Indians—First contact with Europeans—
Early works to 1800.
2. America—Discovery and exploration—
Early works to 1800.
I. Title.

E59.F53W55 2011
970.01—dc22
2011015423

CONTENTS

ILLUSTRATIONS

Figures

Maps

Latin American Originals (LAO) is a series of primary source texts on colonial and nineteenth-century Latin America. LAO volumes are accessible, affordable editions of texts translated into English—most of them for the very first time. The first half-dozen books in the series illuminate aspects of the Spanish conquests during the long century of 1494–1614.

Taken in the chronological order of their primary texts, LAO 7, *Of Cannibals and Kings*, comes first. It presents the very first written attempt to describe the native cultures of the Americas. In the volume, this early ethnography, written by a Catalan named Ramón Pané but surviving only in Italian, is packaged with complementary Spanish texts and placed within the context of the conquest and collapse of the complex societies of the Caribbean islands in the late 1490s. Of the five documents here, three are given new translations and two are published in English for the first time. Together they offer startling new insight into how the first Europeans in the Americas struggled from the very start to conceive a New World.

LAO 2 comes next chronologically. *Invading Guatemala* shows how reading multiple accounts of conquest wars (in this case, Spanish, Nahua, and Maya versions of the Guatemalan conflict of the 1520s) can explode established narratives and suggest a conquest story that is more complicated, disturbing, and revealing. LAO 1, *Invading Colombia*, challenges us to view the difficult Spanish invasion of Colombia in the 1530s as more representative of conquest campaigns than the better-known assaults on the Mexica and Inka empires. LAO 5, *Forgotten Franciscans*, casts light on the spiritual conquest and the conflictive cultural world of the Inquisition in sixteenth-century Mexico. LAO 3, *The Conquest on Trial*, features a fictional embassy of native Americans filing a complaint over the conquest in a court in Spain—the Court of Death. That text, the first theatrical examination of the conquest published in Spain, effectively condensed contemporary debates on colonization into one dramatic package. LAO 4, *Defending the Conquest*, is a spirited, ill-humored, and polemic apologia for the Spanish Conquest written by a lesser-known veteran conquistador and submitted for publication—without success—in 1613.

The source texts to LAO volumes are either archival documents—written in Spanish, Portuguese, or indigenous languages such as Nahuatl, Zapotec, and Maya—or rare books published in the colonial period in their original language (Spanish, Portuguese, Italian, Latin). The contributing authors are historians, anthropologists, art historians, and scholars of literature; they have developed a specialized knowledge that allows them to locate, translate, and present these texts in a way that contributes to scholars' understanding of the period, while also making them readable for students and nonspecialists.

Neil Whitehead is a specialist of such an ilk. His dozen books explore issues of violence and war, shamanism and witchcraft, and the complex cultures and identities of native peoples in Amazonia, Guyana, and the Caribbean. Among those publications are definitive editions of primary source texts by Hans Staden and Sir Walter Ralegh; add to them the brilliant packaging of Pané and others in LAO 5, and Whitehead has pulled off a remarkable hat trick.

—Matthew Restall

ACKNOWLEDGMENTS

Many colleagues have provided insights and comments without which this work would have been the poorer. In particular I want to thank Peter Hulme, Joan-Pau Rubiés, and Margarita Zamora, all extraordinary scholars of the Caribbean and its early texts; their comments on aspects of the manuscript and in response to talks I have given about the colonial texts of primal anthropology in the Americas have proven most helpful in the production of this work. This volume includes the first translations into English of accounts by Rodrigo Figueroa and Rodrigo de Navarrete, as well as retranslations of selections from the better-known texts of Christopher Columbus and Diego Chanca, based on earlier versions by myself and Peter Hulme published in *Wild Majesty* (Oxford University Press, 1992); for these revised versions I bear sole responsibility. However, I am deeply grateful to Giovanna Micarelli for producing the new translation of Ramón Pané's account from the Italian, published for the first time in this volume. Her work was clearly indispensable, and as an anthropologist she brought a particularly relevant understanding of culture and history to that translation. Pané's account, despite its significance as the first extended description of the native peoples of America, had not been directly translated into English from the original for over one hundred years; other translations have started from Spanish translations of the Italian original (see, for example, José Juan Arrom's recent edition: Pané 1999). Neither has it been interpreted in the light of advances in the anthropological understanding of the Caribbean and its peoples that have also taken place in that time. I would therefore also like to thank George Simon and Joseph Frederick, who have given me invaluable and intimate insight into the continuing significance of still living out those primal categories of anthropology that are so prominent in this work, Arawak and Carib. I would also like to thank the Caribbean artist Penny Slinger-Hills for her generous permission to reproduce her original illustrations of indigenous artifacts, which are beautifully accurate representations of the original objects. Her illustrations speak eloquently to the continuing aesthetic force of those objects in a way that commercially available photographs of such collections do not.

Finally, I would like to thank Matthew Restall, the editor of the Latin American Originals Series, for his persistence and patience in bringing this work to fruition. His insightful understanding of the nature of historical documentation from this region and historical period has permitted me to produce a work that, I hope, not only services advanced scholarship but will also be accessible to less specialized audiences. Given the way in which misleading anthropologies, stemming from that primal moment of first encounter, have spilled over into public cultural understanding of the "discovery" of America, gaining access to a wider readership is important. For both these reasons it is to be hoped that this publication will be of value not just within the academy but also to the enduring struggle of native peoples to claim their right to be heard through the historical record of colonialism and its invention of a New World.

The Lords who were subject to these Five Kings were innumerable, and I knew a great many of them; all had an immense number of subjects. . . . When the King Guarionex called him one of his vassals would come to serve him with 16,000 warriors.

—Bartolomé de Las Casas, *The Five Kings of Hispaniola*

They say that this *cacique* claimed that he had talked with Giocauugama, who told him that those who survived him would enjoy their rule for a short time, because dressed people would arrive in their country, who would dominate and kill them, and that they would starve to death. At first they thought that these people had to be the *cannibali*, but . . . they now believe that these are the admiral and the people that he brings.

—Ramón Pané, *The Antiquities of the Indians*

The Caribbean generally and the island of Hispaniola specifically is the linchpin, the pivot point where the old world swung into the new world. If you want the transformation point, if you want the ground zero where the Old World died and the New World began, it's there. . . . The modern world was given rise by what began in the Caribbean.

—Junot Diaz, *Newsweek*, April 3, 2008

Introduction: Of Cannibals and Kings

The Caribbean became the initial scene of the encounter between Europe and the Americas on October 12, 1492, as the fleet of Christopher Columbus first sighted land. Columbus went on to explore the northeast coast of Cuba, where he landed on October 28, as well as the northern coast of Hispaniola in December. When one of the three ships ran aground and had to be abandoned, Columbus, with the permission of the native leader Guacanagari, left thirty-nine men behind and founded the settlement of La Navidad in what is now Haiti. The native population of the island the Spanish called Hispaniola, Aiti in the native language, was therefore the first to negotiate the new political and economic realities that the Europeans imposed, as well as to endure the ecological and demographic consequences of that arrival. The consequence of arrival, for European and Amerindian alike, was the advent of a modernity whose ruins we still inhabit. Perhaps, in all its poverty and urban decay, its prophetic reflection of those states of exception that haunt the contemporary imagination, Haiti is in fact the most modern country in the world. For the discovery was indeed of a "new" world, and it was one in which we were the cannibals and they the kings, as had been prophesied.

The title to this volume—*Of Cannibals and Kings*—thus hints at such an inversion of historically received reality, one I hope is worthy of the phantasmagorical worlds created by Lewis Carroll, who famously employed a similar phrase.[1] But anthropophagy and kingship have been among the earliest and most persistent of modern

---

1. The title may also be familiar to many anthropologists from Marvin Harris's polemical collection of essays, *Cannibals and Kings* (1977), in which he made the rather quixotic suggestion that cannibalism, at least for the Aztecs, was an attempt to offset protein deficiencies. Certainly the idea of "cannibalism" is prominent in the writings collected in this volume, but its elusive meanings and the cultural politics that surrounded the accusation were far more sophisticated and directed to quite different

anthropological issues, as Michel de Montaigne's famous essays "Of Cannibals" and "Of Coaches" well demonstrate (Montaigne 2007). The chivalric Spanish rescuing of a feminized America from the clutches of cannibal savages was a powerful image in its own day, and we might wonder how far in fact we have traveled from that moment and its symbolism. But its anachronistic aspects were certainly part of the rhetorical claims of the French, Dutch, and English as they sought legal and political access to the fabulously profitable relations of production of war and slavery that had been created in this new and marvelous world. The invention of a "new" world thus presented challenges not just of navigation, logistics, finance, politics, law, and so forth, but also of the self-fashioning of Europe itself. Montaigne's *Essais*, not unlike the writings of Bartolomé de Las Casas[2] in the Spanish world, focused on the key issue of who is what—cannibal or king? savage primitive or civilized modern? Caliban or Prospero? Carroll's Walrus and Carpenter talked of many things, including cabbages and kings, a phrase that O. Henry also used in the title of his now largely forgotten 1904 novel set in Central America. Perhaps with conscious irony, one of the native Carib characters in the novel is called Chanca. As will be seen from the writings of Dr. Chanca, companion to Columbus on his second voyage, it was he who firmly associated through ethnological observations the idea that the ethnic identity of "Carib" necessarily entailed "cannibalism."

The documents collected here, and in particular the description of Hispaniola by Ramón Pané, thus reflect the inception of those ideas

---

ends than Harris supposed (Whitehead 2008). Nonetheless, Harris himself might well have approved of the attempt to read the politics of culture implicit in the accusation and the discussion of the connections between power and imagination in this volume; or he might not have.

2. Bartolomé de Las Casas (1484–1566) is famous for having spoken out against the Spanish colonists' enslavement of and brutality toward native peoples, which he had witnessed directly. His work *Brevísima relación de la destruición de las Indias* (A Short Account of the Destruction of the Indies; 1542; published 1552) conveys a very negative picture of Spanish destruction of native cultures through the Caribbean, Central America, and the coast of Venezuela. Las Casas came to Hispaniola as a colonist in 1502. He was ordained as a priest in 1510, and became an advocate for the Indians as fellow humans, and for a policy of evangelization rather than enslavement. (It is important to note, however, that Las Casas initially favored importing Africans as slaves, in lieu of New World populations; he later renounced this idea.) After joining the Dominican Order in 1522, he went to Cuba and later to Mexico as a missionary. In 1544 he was appointed the first bishop of Chiapas.

and in so doing provide the basis for the primal anthropology that developed over subsequent centuries. The first descriptions of the Caribbean by Columbus and Chanca, and the description of Hispaniola by Ramón Pané and the deposition of Figueroa, are the key texts through which such ideas were formed and promulgated. The later description of the coast of Guyana by Navarrete then shows how such ideas traveled to the southern continent.

In the islands of the Caribbean the colonial cannibals' consumption of the native kings was brief and brutal, especially in Hispaniola, Jamaica, and Puerto Rico, where the native population all but disappeared within a few decades. Longer-lasting and more convoluted conflicts occurred in the Lesser Antilles, whose inhabitants offered stout resistance to a succession of colonial powers, as did the native societies of Tierra Firme (the continental mainland). These more extended interactions produced a wide range of novel political and economic responses on the part of the native population. Alongside exterminations and epidemics new political and military formations arose. The ethnopolitical identities referred to by the Spanish as *caribe* and *aruaca* were the primary expression of this process in the Caribbean and northeastern South America region (Whitehead 1988, 1995, 2002a). For these reasons, none of the indigenous polities in the islands or the coastal mainland that were extant in 1492 survived unscathed. Even where contacts were not direct, the impact of the Europeans on regional trade and alliance systems was fundamental, inducing change among groups well before they ever encountered the invaders directly. Such a pattern of effect outrunning its cause was also seen in the spread of European epidemic diseases, which not only proved particularly lethal to native populations, but also provoked a rapid and widespread migration away from the epicenters of disease dispersion. Although the virulence of diseases was enhanced by the geographic constraints on island populations, all apparent population loss in the Caribbean and proximate regions of South America cannot be explained by disease; migrations by sea toward the continent were another factor.

Within eight years of Columbus's first arrival, the Spanish Crown sent a royal governor, Francisco de Bobadilla, to try to stabilize the nascent colony on Hispaniola, where Columbus, his family, and their opponents had all but destroyed the indigenous population in a series of brutal military campaigns against both indigenous opposition and the dissenting Spanish factions (Wilson 1990, 74–110). The critical moment in these events was a large-scale military confrontation in 1495 between the Europeans and the natives of the valley of Maguá (or La Vega Real), the largest and most densely populated native province on the island. Here barely two hundred men faced the combined forces of the principal *caciques*[3] of Hispaniola, numbering tens of thousands of warriors. However, the military technology and organization of the Europeans, which included armored cavalry, steel weapons, guns, and attack dogs, devastated the native warriors, whose leaders were captured and tortured to death. Out of this destruction the *cacique* Guarionex emerged to mediate European demands for food, labor, and, above all, gold. By 1497, following on famine and the first outbreaks of epidemic disease, this appeasement ended when Francisco de Roldán induced various *caciques,* including Guarionex, to support his opposition to the Columbus family. But Bartolomé Columbus forestalled any action by a night attack on Guarionex's villages to seize the rebel *caciques,* most of whom were executed. Guarionex himself was allowed to live, but functioned essentially as a tool of the Columbus family until his death by shipwreck en route to Spain in 1502.

By 1500 most of the complex native polities of Hispaniola had ceased to operate, and, following Ponce de Léon's conquest of Puerto Rico in the early 1500s, the kingdoms of the Greater Antilles had effectively collapsed. The few native survivors of this first decade or so of European occupation were incorporated into the burgeoning colonial settlements of the region, and the need for labor was answered by the importation of black Africans as slaves. What percentage of the aboriginal population either fled the Greater Antilles or died there is open to question, but the overall consequence, as the colonial processes that had unfolded on Hispaniola repeated themselves in Cuba, Jamaica, the Lucayas, and Puerto Rico, was the near-complete disappearance of indigenous societies from the islands. However, in Puerto Rico, which was proximate both physically and culturally to Hispaniola and where Ponce de Léon first led an expedition of reconnaissance in 1508 (CDI 31, 283–87), native resistance on the island itself, though short-lived, was fierce, being supported by *caribes* (indigenous insurgents) from the smaller islands of

---

3. An Hispanicized native term for chieftains, nobles, lords, or kings.

Lesser Antilles. In fact, attacks by Amerindians on the Spanish in Puerto Rico continued throughout the sixteenth century as alliances emerged between the Lesser Antilles *caribes* and the native populations dispersed and driven out by Ponce de Léon's conquest and other Spanish occupations of the northerly islands. By contrast, little resistance was encountered in the Lucayas, the most northerly of the Caribbean islands, where the population was simply "harvested" by slavers from 1509 to 1512 (CDI 31, 438–39). The emergence of *caribes*, from the very inception of the European presence in the Caribbean, as an enduring source of resistance to colonial control is thus closely linked to the way in which their characterization as "cannibals," from the first reports of Columbus up to the present day, was inextricably joined to the self-serving interests of the colonial rule.

Few records have been left concerning the occupation of Jamaica, which was initiated by Diego Columbus and completed by Juan de Esquivel in 1509. Apparently the natives were not evangelized but were put to hard labor in the production of foodstuffs, cloth, and hammocks (Las Casas 1909, bk. 2, chap. 56). When the new governor, Francisco de Garay, took over from Esquivel in 1515, the royal factor, Pedro de Mazuelo, complained of the tiny number of natives left on the island, and confidently predicted their total disappearance within a couple of years (CDI 1, 258).

Columbus had surveyed the coast of Cuba during his first voyage, but official interest did not manifest itself again until 1508, when the royal governor of Hispaniola, Nicolás de Ovando, sent Sebastián de Ocampo to circumnavigate the island. Rumors of gold quickly followed (CDI 31, 388). In 1511 a license to occupy Cuba was given to Diego Velázquez de Cuéllar, a veteran of the conquest on Hispaniola. Cuéllar assembled three hundred troops on the southwestern peninsula of Hispaniola and was joined on Cuba by troops fresh from the conquest of Jamaica. A further contingent from Hispaniola included the future Amerindian apologist Bartolomé de Las Casas, for whom this military campaign was to prove a critical experience in the formation of his negative views on the European treatment of the native population. With brutal efficiency the two parties of invaders had overrun the island completely by March of the following year (CDI 32, 369–72).

The rapid conquests in these islands of the Greater Antilles contrast strongly with the situation in the Lesser Antilles, which became a refuge not just for native populations, but also for the *cimarrónes*[4] (escaped black slaves). Puerto Rico emerged as the southern frontier of Spanish settlement in the Caribbean islands, with the Lesser Antilles becoming occupied only in the seventeenth century, not by Spain but by Spain's imperial rivals, the French, Dutch, and English. During the hiatus, the native populations of the Lesser Antilles were able to take advantage of their position on the main shipping lanes between Europe and America to practice a profitable trade with the European vessels that stopped to replenish their drinking water and supplies after the Atlantic crossing (Hulme and Whitehead 1992, 45–80). Relations with the Spanish were invariably hostile, and the farms and ranches of Puerto Rico were frequently raided by the *caribes*, who, it was suspected, held not just African and European captives (including the son of the governor of Puerto Rico) but also a vast treasure of gold and silver taken from wrecked and plundered shipping. The issue of the *caribes* therefore remained a preoccupation of the Puerto Rican colonists, who continued to collect evidence of their lawlessness and "cannibalism" in the hope of persuading the Crown to permit the slaving of the Lesser Antilles (Hulme and Whitehead 1992, 38–44). But Spanish imperial ambition had turned its attention to the wonders of the Incan and Aztec empires, as well as the rich plunder to be had all along the Central American isthmus. The struggle of the Puerto Rican colonists with the *caribes* little troubled metropolitan Spain until the *caribes* made alliance with the French, English, and Dutch in the seventeenth century.

The Political Economy of Conquest

The Antillean archipelago was not only the first locale for the violent encounter between Europeans and Amerindians; it was also the first American space to be transformed into "colonies of exploitation" (Sued Badillo 1995). The available gold deposits in the Greater Antilles quickly made them the epicenter of an ever-expanding economic core within the larger Caribbean region. Gold became the driving

---

4. The term *cimarrón* appears to derive from the Spanish *cima* ("summit"), since escaped slaves habitually sought refuge in the relatively impassable hill and mountain ranges that lie just beyond the coastal strip on many of the islands throughout the Caribbean region, as well as the Venezuelan coast.

force behind a dynamic and diversified economic zone that traded in slaves, foodstuffs, pearls, imported goods, cattle, salt, and exotic woods. Columbus's exaggerated assessment of the region's worth had become true after all, even if he did not live long enough to see it. The significance of Caribbean gold shipments must be appreciated from the perspective of a European economy that had almost exhausted its supplies of that strategic metal. By 1515 the three islands of Hispaniola, Puerto Rico, and Cuba, in that order of importance, were shipping gold to Spain on a regular basis and so stimulating the peopling and exploration of the wider region. Hispaniola was responsible for half of the total of these shipments. These mining economies typically had only basic technologies and an intermittent food supply with very little capital investment. But because they were supported by abundant, cheap slave labor, which could be replenished by raiding native settlements, and because gold was so important to the Spanish Crown, the supply kept flowing.

Amerindian slavery had begun with Columbus himself as a means to finance his own voyages and the costs of administering the first colony of Hispaniola. In time Columbus was responsible for the enslavement and exportation of some two thousand Amerindians to Spain as war captives. His son Diego was appointed as governor of the Indies just as a serious labor shortage became evident in Hispaniola; as a result, Diego Columbus was responsible for the shaping of the slave policy to be followed.[5]

The slaving was at its most intense between the years 1512 and 1542. Alonso Suazo, writing from Hispaniola in 1518, reported that some fifteen thousand slaves had been captured from the Caribbean islands, producing a chaotic situation with consequences for the whole region. In 1545 the government of Hispaniola admitted to the

5. At first the outlying islands were targeted and soon depopulated; according to Las Casas, forty thousand slaves were taken out of the Lucayas alone (1875–76, 2:349). Quoting Peter Martyr, Las Casas gives the number of Amerindian slaves resettled throughout the Caribbean early in the century as 1.2 million. Those numbers may be statistically unreliable, but their political significance should not be lost. What is important to understand is that the demographic collapse of the large islands was offset during the mining period by a very large and efficient repopulation effort involving much of the Caribbean, both the islands and the encircling coastlines. Certainly, production figures for the period attest to a sustained process in spite of the high mortality rate of the native population of Hispaniola, which can only be explained by a constant replenishment of the local labor forces. Slaves were also taken from Florida, Mexico, Central America, Colombia, Venezuela, and the Orinoco and Guyana coast.

existence of five thousand Amerindian slaves. Given that Hispaniola
and Puerto Rico were the main sugar exporters from America, maintaining this ascendancy for many years, the actual numbers would
have been considerably higher (Sued Badillo 1995). Las Casas cited
the coastal regions of Venezuela and Trinidad as the principal source
of the slave traffic to Hispaniola and to Cuba. The pearl islands,
Margarita, Coche, and Cubagua, lying just off the coast of Venezuela,
were the main staging ports for this traffic, underlining the significance of the interactions of *aruacas* (native allies) with the colonists
on Margarita, as described by Rodrigo de Navarrete (see Document
5). Indeed, the strength of this alliance in the second half of the
sixteenth century may have been a primary reason why most slaves
taken to the Caribbean islands in this period came from the Venezuelan littoral and the Atlantic coast south of the Orinoco River.[6] *Caribe*
opposition to both the Spaniards and *aruacas* needs to be understood
in that light, since it made alliance with the *aruacas*, particularly the
Lokono of the Guyanese Atlantic coast region, critical for the slavers.
Only in the context of the emergence of the ethnopolitical groupings of *caribes* and *aruacas* can the writings of this period, and its
historical outcomes, be properly understood (Whitehead 1995). The
caribes were initially found throughout the Lesser Antillean islands,
like Dominica, and they were always viewed as a source of slaves for
the colonial economies. Occasionally slaves taken from the Amazon
region are also reported, and the map drawn to accompany Rodrigo
de Navarrete's *Relación de las Provincia de los Indios Llaman Aruacas* displays the first European knowledge of the fluvial connection
of the Amazon and Orinoco watershed. The map text indicates that
it was an *aruaca*, a chief called Jaime, who had communicated this
knowledge and led a Spanish expedition into the interior to show
them the route.

6. Oviedo y Baños wrote that only eighty-two towns with very little population
existed in the whole province of the Venezuelan coast, many of the coastal inhabitants
having fled to the interior (Oviedo y Baños 1965, 13, 80). The Orinoco and Atlantic coastal regions are also frequently identified as a staging area for slave raiding:
"Among manie other trades those *Spaniards* used in *Canoas* to passe to the rivers . . .
on the south side of the mouth of *Orenoque*, and there buie women and children from
the *Canibals*, which are of that barbarous nature, . . . herebuie the Spaniards make
great profit, for buying a maid of 12 or 13 yeeres for three or fower hatchets, they
sell them again at *Marguerita* . . . for 50 and 100 pesos, which is so many crownes"
(Ralegh 1997, 152–53).

The role of the *aruacas*, in conjunction with the Spanish, in displacing existing native groups as well as directing Spanish slaving and raiding against their selected enemies has been obscured by the persistent reference to the "cannibalism" of the *caribes;* in Spanish writings this occlusion was no doubt partly intentional. The testimony given to the Englishman Lawrence Keymis by one displaced native ruler indicates that the political choice of being *aruaca* also had its consequences. On the arrival of his fleet off the coast at the Caw River (French Guiana), Keymis writes, at first he could get no one to come aboard, since they thought them to be Spanish. Eventually the *cacique* Wareo was persuaded, who "declared unto us, that he was lately chased by the *Spanish* from Moruca, one of the neighbouring rivers to . . . *Orenoque:* and that having burnt his own houses, and destroyed his fruites and gardens, he had left his countrey and townes to be possessed by the *Arwaccas,* who are a vagabound nation of *Indians,* which finding no certaine place of abode of their own, do for the most part serve and follow the *Spaniards"* (Keymis 1596, 4).

The legal framework laid down by the Spanish Crown allowed for unrestricted slaving of those deemed "cannibals." This was the reason for *The Deposition of Rodrigo Figueroa on the Islands of the Barbarous Caribes* (1520; AGI *Justicia* 47, fols. 1–59, CDI *XI:32*), which is included in this volume. Figueroa ethnologically mapped regions where *caribes* might be captured and where *guatiaos* (defined officially as "domestic and tame and friends of the Christians and subject to the service of their highness"; see also Sued Badillo 2003, 261–62) or *aruacas* were. The pattern of *caribe* resistance to the Spanish and their allies the *aruaca* should be interpreted against this backdrop of legal provision and economic interests. The politics of raiding and slaving among the other native groups, all of whom were faced with rapid and dynamic change, was likewise founded on the way in which the categories of colonial ethnology were being deployed politically. Modern anthropology and history have been slow to appreciate this crucial aspect of primal anthropology in the Caribbean.[7] Columbus's

7. The distinction between ethnology and anthropology used here is that ethnology is concerned principally with the analysis and interpretation of particular social groups, especially when ethnically organized ("tribes"). Anthropology, a more recent intellectual construct and the basis of an academic profession only since the nineteenth century, by contrast is inherently comparative and aims to synthesize and interpret

observations were not the disinterested scientific notes of an "explorer"; he in fact elaborated an ethnographic proposal for enslaving the native population that was intended to defray the cost of future explorations and pay for the administrative burden of the first colony of Hispaniola. This primal anthropological criterion for distinguishing one supposed type of Amerindian from another was then widely propagated during the following years by Columbus's friends and lobbyists, including Diego Chanca, whose writings are excerpted in this volume. Together they effectively disseminated throughout Europe the notion that cannibal *caribes* inhabited the Caribbean, as the very place-name suggests. Although this early imagery little benefited Columbus himself, it was eagerly deployed by the colonizers who followed. The first royal decree allowing for the enslavement of the "cannibals" was issued by Queen Isabella in 1503 to encourage new self-financing explorations. As a result, the *conquistadores* Cristobal Guerra, Alonso de Ojeda, and Amerigo Vespucci, who had lobbied for the reinstatement of slavery, all became involved in commercial expeditions to the Caribbean and Orinoco region.[8]

In 1510 the *cacique* Agueybana led a native uprising in which over half of the two hundred Spaniards on Puerto Rico were killed. Following reports of *caribes* being involved, the Crown issued a new decree ordering general war on the *caribes* and allowing for their unrestricted enslavement. This decree contained the first legal definition of a *caribe* territory and association of the *caribes* with the ethnological marker of "cannibalism." Diego Columbus was primarily responsible for this new delineation of *caribe* settlements; he advocated widening the *caribe* frontier to the South American continent. However, his suggestion was eventually rejected by the Spanish Crown, possibly conscious of the hidden agenda behind it.

---

culture on a global scale. Ethnography is the methodology of direct, eyewitness observation that supports both these intellectual projects. It is necessarily participatory to some degree, as this is what provides the opportunity for firsthand observation. Clearly, in the context of conquest, "participation" may come to mean destruction and violence, but the observations arising from this are not epistemologically any less credible for the purposes of ethnography, an issue that has become a matter of grave concern to many contemporary anthropologists (Whitehead 2009).

8. But in the edict of 1503 the "cannibal islands" did not exactly match Columbus's earlier geography. The new places included such far-flung locales as Cartagena region and the Gulf of Urabá. Columbus's classification was modified to enable these business ventures make a profit in the New World.

This underlines the extent to which Spanish royal policy was itself severely constrained by the practical ethnologies that the colonists in the field of conquest generated. The eloquent text of an educated historian and priest like Bartolomé de Las Casas was apt to be trumped by the field reports, in the form of judicial documents and routine government correspondence, generated by the firsthand eyewitnesses "at play in the fields of the lord." The political nature of ethnic and geographical identification is apparent from the fact that Guadeloupe was not included among the new *caribe* islands, despite being densely populated and despite the fact that Columbus had personally visited it and described the inhabitants as "cannibals." Guadeloupe had been set aside for private settlement and would have been devastated and left worthless if opened to slaving.

In subsequent years the mining economies plunged the eastern Caribbean and costal Venezuela into chaos. Slave armadas were organized and sent against different islands, sometimes nearly depopulating them. In the process the Spanish Crown required that the capture of *caribes* had to have "legal foundations." In effect, this meant that the governor of Hispaniola was being instructed to supply the Spanish Crown with the cultural information to justify the crude political distinctions promulgated from Spain, just as the early modern "discovery" of witches throughout Europe, which paralleled this "discovery" of cannibals, was an ethnographic exercise partly serviced by the information gathered through systematic torture.[9] Nonetheless, this process produced intellectual debate and political unrest in elite circles of the Spanish Court and church, as did awareness of the growing death rate of the Amerindians in the New World. In response, in 1515 the Crown appointed Francisco de Vallejo to investigate and classify the Amerindians of the mainland to determine who were *caribes* and who were not, but slavers blocked the inquiry (Otte 1977, 128). In 1519 Judge Antonio de la Gama in Puerto Rico was commissioned to determine the extent of *caribe* territory, but without result. In later years, as part of the agreement with the Crown to allow missionary personnel into the mainland of

---

9. Among the most influential manuals on witch finding, Scot's *Discoverie* was highly ethnographic, being a compendia of local and folk beliefs and practices that were designed to allow better discrimination between the harmless and the evil, a form of "Spiritual Terrain System," a forebear of the modern U.S. Army's "Human Terrain System" which sorts friend from foe in Afghanistan and Iraq (Whitehead 2009).

South America, Bartolomé de Las Casas was also asked to contribute to this emerging colonial ethnology, and his response is instructive: "If ordered to find out which people and in what provinces human flesh was eaten, then to say: 'I declare such a province to be eaters of human flesh and those do not want friendship with the Spaniards,' the result would be the captain with his 120 men would simply make war on them and enslave those taken alive" (Las Casas 1909, bk. 3, 371; quoted in Sued Badillo 1995). Las Casas thus rejected the project that was finally carried out by Rodrigo de Figueroa, at the time a newly appointed justice of Hispaniola and the proud owner of a brand new sugar mill. Figueroa's final report (1520; translated and published for the first time in this volume) opened the mainland to slave raiding as the labor force of the mining islands was declining rapidly due to epidemics. Put simply, his report meant that almost a quarter of a century after the conquest had begun, the fate of native peoples still hung on the ethnic distinctions founded on behavior favoring or resisting the Spanish conquest.

The Spanish Crown finally decreed a prohibition against Amerindian slavery in the "New Laws" of 1542. However, local slavers, often supported by local politicians, easily got around the legalities, and in 1547 *caribes* were again declared subject to slaving (Sued Badillo 1978). In this way the Spanish continued to adopt native categories into their distorted ethnologies in order to service the needs of colonial conquest, and Amerindians continued to be actively involved in this process, practically and intellectually. As with Christopher Columbus, identification of *caribes* always involved information claimed to have been supplied by Amerindians. Certainly the European presence polarized many political allegiances amongst Amerindians, and, as elsewhere in the Caribbean and South America (see also Sued Badillo 2003, 261–62), the conquest could not have proceeded without the active alliance of native armies and political leaders. Amerindians allied to the Spanish were initially termed *guatiao*. As the southern continent was opened up by slavers, this term was superseded by *aruaca* due to the increasing political importance to Spanish colonial plans of the "Aruacas" (Arawaks or Lokono in their own language) as described in Navarrete's *Relación* (Document 5; AGI *Justicia* 47). Like *caribe*, *aruaca* implied a political and social orientation, ranging from alliance to submissiveness. *Guatiaos*, and later those termed *aruacas*, actively participated in ethnic soldiering for the Spanish conquest.[10] Las Casas understood this process very well when he wrote, "*caribes,* that was the term that the Spanish used to make free people into slaves" (1909, 380). The filter of *caribe* and *guatiao* or *aruaca* therefore dominates the cultural politics of primal anthropology in the vast majority of early materials, beginning with Columbus. Since the politics of representation are mainly evidenced in the ethnologically sparse reports of judges, lawmakers, and other bureaucrats or self-interested parties, the account of Hispaniola and its native peoples written by Ramón Pané, significant in its own right, takes on even greater significance as the last glimpse of the native Caribbean world uninflected by the colonial politics of difference.

The Ethnology of Conquest

In a general context of armed invasion and conquest, the first encounters with the natives of the islands loom largest in the historiography of the region and in the ethnological schema of anthropologies subsequent to the first encounters, both colonial and modern. This was because the *caribe/aruaca* distinction was used to ethnologically configure broad swaths of the mainland population, as shown in Figueroa's deposition (Document 4). Ethnological informa-tion was thus crucial to the colonial project. The writings collected in

10. Sued Badillo perfectly evokes this process: "The *guatiaos* rapidly internalized Spanish jargon and contributed to its dissemination. In the interrogation of the crew members of a slave expedition to Venezuela sponsored by members of the Hispaniola élite around 1519, one of the witnesses declared 'that in the Gulf of Paria they rescued from the *guatiao* Indians that are in peace 70 or 80 slaves and that among them there are no *caribes* that clearly can be taken as *caribe,* but that the said *guatiao* have them as slaves and the Indians call them *caribes* when they are angry with them.' Another witness was asked how he knew that the slaves were *caribes,* to which he answered 'that the said *guatiaos* told him they were *caribes* when they were sold'. Pressed on to have him answer how he could tell if they were *caribes* or not, the witness simply said that he did not know. Witness Anton Garcia in the inquiry held by Rodrigo de Figueroa concerning the identity of the inhabitants of Trinidad answered 'and that what he knows of it is inhabited by *guatiaos* and they are honored to be so and run away and spit if they are called *caribes.* [Further on he insisted that the Indians of Trinidad were not *caribes* and added] and neither are the others who travel in those parts, were it not for some that with malice, and in order to gain a piece in the said island say that they are *caribes*'" (Sued Badillo 1995, 74, quoting AGI, *Justicia* 47). Certainly, then, the political meaning of the term was well understood by Amerindians throughout the region.

this volume reflect precisely this role of providing anthropological intelligence on populations for purposes of their governance or conquest, and the relationship between such intelligence and military-political ambition has remained fraught right up to the present day.[11] These writings also reflect an increasing codification of subject matter and of the categories through which the native population was understood, which resulted in a key distinction between, perhaps unsurprisingly, tractable and intractable populations, stemming from Columbus's ethnological distinction between the *caribes* and the rest of the people of the Caribbean. The selection in this volume of passages from his *Letter* and extracts from the *Journal* of his first voyage to America is crucial to appreciating this process of ethnological codification. It will be apparent that in fact the distinction between the *caribes* and others is far from certain in these writings but continues to gain significance as the Spanish occupation of the Caribbean islands takes hold.

When Christopher Columbus (1451–1506) sailed east from Spain in the late summer of 1492, he hoped to find Asia. Instead his fleet arrived in the Caribbean. On the return voyage Columbus wrote a letter (included in this volume as Document 1a) to Luis de Santángel, clerk to the Spanish sovereigns Ferdinand and Isabella, who had partly financed his voyage. Published in Barcelona in 1493, the *Letter*, in Latin translation, became the main way through which Columbus's voyage became known in Europe. It ran to nine editions before the end of 1494 and was published in many cities outside Spain. According to Columbus's account, at first contact both the Spanish and the indigenous population were cautious but curious; gifts were exchanged and hospitality offered and accepted. The emphasis in the *Letter* is on the charm of the islands and the variety of their natural resources, especially precious metals. The people are described as naked and timid, lacking weapons, almost infantile. But the *Letter* also hints at the existence of more threatening people from an island that is "Carib," whom Columbus suspects of being man-eaters. It is here that the long and vicious association of "Caribs" and "cannibals" has its origin.

---

11. *Anthropological Intelligence* is also the title of a book by David Price (2008) on academic-military collaboration in the twentieth century, a topic currently much debated within academia as a result of the various programs that the U.S. military has funded to recruit anthropologists to assist the wars in Iraq and Afghanistan (see also Whitehead 2009 and note 24 below).

Columbus wrote his *Journal* (Document 1b) on most evenings of that first voyage. He probably intended it for the Spanish monarchs, to whom a copy was later given. However, both the original version and the royal copy were lost, and all that survives is an extended summary made by the Spanish historian Bartolomé de Las Casas, which refers to Columbus as "the Admiral." Before its loss the journal was used extensively by historians like Las Casas and Peter Martyr d'Anghiera[12] and by Columbus's brother and biographer, Ferdinand. Las Casas's summary was itself mislaid and not published until the middle of the nineteenth century. Its fate was thus not unlike that of Ramón Pané's account, which was commissioned by Columbus and likewise survived only in various translated and/or redacted forms.[13] Apparent contradictions of fact and interpretation are evident in the *Journal*, suggesting a text that had not been extensively rewritten.

Diego Alvarez Chanca, a doctor to the Spanish sovereigns, was appointed the surgeon for Columbus's fleet. During Columbus's second voyage in 1494, the same voyage on which Ramón Pané arrived in the New World, he wrote his *Report* to the municipality of Seville, where he was born. Chanca's account (Document 2) is widely recognized as the principal source for that voyage, and together with Pané's account it proved an important justification for Columbus's claims about and actions towards the native population. Although Chanca was not on the first voyage, in describing the progress of the second voyage through the Lesser Antilles he was certainly influenced by Columbus's own expectations. Chanca was quick to identify human remains, perhaps of funerary origin, as firm evidence of the cannibal propensities of the *caribes*. Chanca develops this initial distinction with various ethnological observations that ultimately allow

---

12. The Italian chronicler Peter Martyr d'Anghera (1457–1526) collected and published accounts of explorations in Central and South America in a series of "decades." These were published together in 1530 as *De Orbe Novo*.

13. Perkins (2007, 1–10) provides a useful summary of the editorial history of Pané's manuscript, in the context of a study of José Juan Arrom's 1974 Spanish-language edition. She also makes the valuable observation that "the *Relación* is the product of the process by which reading creates meaning, which is then revealed and can ONLY be revealed, by creating or writing a new text to set in juxtaposition to the very object or experience each reader was investigating. That new text, while it may subsume the previous one as subaltern, also maps out the autoethnography of the reader, now writer of the interpretation that becomes the next text" (8; see also Buzard 2003).

him to declare unequivocally that "the way of life of these *caribe* people is bestial."

Although quite different from these journals and letters, Ramón Pané's account of the natives of Hispaniola also had its origin in ethnological delineation as a prelude to conquest. Pané was commissioned by Columbus himself to reside among the native people of Hispaniola and provide a description of their customs and habits. The resulting document, newly translated for this volume (Document 3), has had a very complex history, but is the most extensive eyewitness account we have of the people of Hispaniola, who would disappear soon after the Spanish occupation of the island, either killed by war and disease, absorbed into the emerging colonial society, or fleeing from the epicenter of contact. While "caribes" are continuously mentioned throughout the literature of colonialism in the Caribbean and northern South America, it is only through the earliest accounts, particularly Pané's, that we have any information at all about the indigenous population of Hispaniola. For this reason Pané's *Antiquities* needs a more extensive contextualization than any other of the materials in this volume. It is both more obscure, because of its fraught history of editing and publication, and more illuminating, both because of the ethnographic nature of Pané's stance as author and because of the simple lack of other sources relating to this time and place.

But before a closer examination of Pané's account, we should mention the later writings of Rodrigo de Figueroa (1520) and Rodrigo de Navarrete (1550), which also appear in this volume (Documents 4 and 5). Like Pané's *Antiquities*, these writings deal not with *caribes* but with the *aruacas*. The term *guatiao*, although still used by Figueroa, was increasingly restricted to the Caribbean islands alone, and disappeared altogether as the alliance with the *aruacas* came to dominate Spanish regional policy. Neither term really designates a distinct ethnic population. Rather, they were characterizations based on how such populations were seen in relation to Spanish ambitions. In fact, unlike the population of Hispaniola, which although nominally *guatiao* had fiercely resisted Spanish colonization, the *aruacas* emerged in the sixteenth century as firm supporters of the Spanish, even accepting black slaves from them to work *aruaca* tobacco plantations at the mouth of the Orinoco. In this way there was a rewriting of the political history of the initial occupation through downplaying resistance on Hispaniola, as well as a continuing policy of political discrimination, deriving from the ethnological frameworks created by Figueroa and Navarrete.

The result has been that those initial observations by Europeans of the native population have become enshrined in the literature concerning the Caribbean region.[14] Unfortunately, much recent scholarship has continued to reproduce these ideas. Part of the purpose of this volume, therefore, is to make evident the way in which early European writing and policy in the Caribbean was a way of re-forming the political and cultural realities of the indigenous population. Consequently, our perceptions of the native Caribbean are heavily prejudiced by the distinction, first made by Columbus, between the fearsome *caribes* of the Lesser Antilles and the tractable *aruaca* or *guatiao*, later known as Taíno,[15] populations of the Greater Antilles and Atlantic coast of the continent. This fallacious distinction was generalized ultimately across the whole of the northern part of the South American continent, with continuing implications for contemporary anthropology (Whitehead 2002a).

Recent scholarship on the native population of the Caribbean has begun to make good that deficiency, but the tenacity of this ethnological dualism partly stems from the historical reason that it was directly adopted into Spanish colonial law, which defined *caribes* as any and all natives who opposed Spanish occupation in the Caribbean (Hulme and Whitehead 1992; Sued-Badillo 1978; Whitehead 1995). The result was that *caribes* were discovered on the continent as well as the islands, and the policy of directly enslaving those who could not be brought within the colonial system of *repartimiento* (a forced redistribution of native lands and peoples) was applied widely. The political orientation of native societies over such issues thus strongly conditioned their political responses to all Europeans. The diplomacy initially exercised toward the *caciques* of Hispaniola strongly contrasts with the summary military invasions of Puerto Rico, Trinidad,

14. Most notably in the *Handbook of South American Indians* (see Rouse 1948), as well as in the recently reissued history *The Early Spanish Main* by Carl Sauer (2008; originally published in 1966).

15. The term *Taíno* as an ethnic ascription, although derived from native terminology, was only coined in the nineteenth century by C. S. Rafinesque (1836), lending a spurious authority to the ethnographic dualism of the early Spanish accounts. A number of other terms, such as *ciboney, ciguayo, bohio, aïtij, boriqua,* as well as the titles of *caciques,* occur in the early sources and may have carried ethnic implications.

and the Venezuelan littoral, the early hunting grounds for slavers seeking labor to replace the wasted population of the Greater Antilles. Ethnological expectations and definitions became critical political factors, as is shown in the great debate between Bartolomé de Las Casas and Juan Ginés Sepúlveda concerning the humanity, rationality, and governance of the New World population.[16]

These ethnological definitions were also responsive to the unfolding needs of the emergent colonial system. For example, in the case of the *caribes* it was finally necessary for the Spanish Crown to dispatch a special legal mission, under the *licenciado* (magistrate) Rodrigo de Figueroa, to make an evaluation as to the *caribe* nature of the native populations of the Caribbean islands and Venezuelan littoral. Figueroa's deposition of 1520 indicates that this process was highly political, in that populations were assigned to the *caribe* category in a way that served the interests of the mine owners, planters, and slavers of Hispaniola and other Spanish enclaves in the region. Figueroa's classification was therefore only tangentially related to substantive ethnological issues, being obsessed with the practice of cannibalism. This is shown both by the fact that populations that were previously *guatiao* could become *caribe* and by Figueroa's own usage of the term *caribe,* in which the eating of human flesh is only one, although the most persistent, of the criteria he cites for so classifying a population. Perhaps not surprisingly, neither the judicial report of Figueroa nor the detailed information supplied by Ramón Pané was sufficient to provide adequate support for policy making by the Spanish Crown. Not only were the ethnological judgments of the colonists often self-serving, but the colonial impact itself resulted in

16. The Spanish theologian Juan Ginés de Sepúlveda (1489–1573) was the adversary of Bartolomé de Las Casas in the so-called Valladolid Debate in 1550, which was concerned with the ethical and theological basis of the Spanish conquests in America. Organized by Charles V (grandson of Ferdinand and Isabella), the debate in fact was not a verbal dispute but a series of publications by the protagonists on these topics. Sepúlveda took the view that the Spanish Crown had a just cause in seeking to colonize and evangelize the peoples of territories of America. He based his opinion on the prevalent juridical idea, derived from Aristotle, that, in a context where the indigenous peoples were not capable of self-governance, such dominion by advanced Christian nations was part of a "natural" law and order of things. He cited human sacrifice, cannibalism, and an absence of governmental institutions as evidence of this incapacity, as well as biblical and classical texts. Las Casas utilized the same sources in his counterargument, claiming that Christ had died to redeem all the peoples of the world, including those who were ignorant of Christianity (see also Pagden 1982).

the emergence of new political groupings among the native population, reflecting these new political realties of ethnic and ethnological profiling. As the original population of Hispaniola drained away, not only were the colonists forced to turn to the African slave trade for a supply of labor, but they were also, to offset the increasing resistance and depredation from *caribes,* forced to seek out new alliances among the still little-known peoples of the continent (Whitehead and Alemán 2009).

Preeminent among these new potential allies, and culturally and linguistically related to the peoples of the islands, were the Lokono. Probably the first direct contact between Europeans and the Lokono did not come until the 1530s, when a Spanish fleet under the command of Diego de Ordaz, with orders to explore and settle the Orinoco region, lost one of its vessels off the Atlantic coast south of the Orinoco. Many tales circulated in subsequent years as to what had become of the crew and colonists, including suggestions that they had largely survived the shipwreck and were still living among indigenous groups. Sometime in the 1540s this notion was dramatically confirmed by the appearance of an unnamed *morisco*[17] in the Spanish settlement of Margarita, center of the Spanish pearl-diving industry off the coast of Venezuela. The *morisco* claimed to be one of those survivors and to have been living ever since with other Spanish who were rescued by *aruacas* of the Berbice and Corentyn rivers. This incident is important not only for the historiography of Spanish colonization but also for the likely implication that the *aruacas,* principally consisting of the Lokono of the Guyana coastal savannas, had consciously developed their knowledge of these strange colonizers through pursuing all kinds of contacts with them. The previously untranslated document of Rodrigo de Navarrete,[18] *Relación de las provincias y naciones que los Indios llaman Aruacas,* is included here for the important light it sheds on the continuing processes of indigenous response to European colonization and how they were shaped by the fallacious and self-interested ethnological claims initiated by

17. *Moriscos* (Spanish, meaning "Moor-like") were nominally Catholic residents of Spain and Portugal with Islamic heritage. The term was used pejoratively for one suspected of still believing in Islam.

18. Little is known of Navarrete except what he tells us in his *Relación,* according to Pablo Ojer's discussion (1966, 203–4), but the ethnological and linguistic information he supplies certainly accords with later, more detailed descriptions of the Lokono Arawaks.

Columbus and elaborated by Figueroa and Navarrete. As will be evident from the *Relación*, the *aruacas* were quite aware of the negative imagery surrounding the ethnic ascription *caribe*, and therefore the need to clearly distance themselves from that ascription. The native population was polarized around the question of how to meet and deal with the European invaders. Some favored appeasement, others confrontation, but no single strategy was successful over time, and actual responses were often highly variable, even within the same village or household.

Navarrette's *Relación* was relatively unknown in its day and so was not recruited to the kinds of polemical, juridical, political, and cultural roles that Ramón Pané's *Antiquities* was.[19] Moreover, if the *Antiquities* is the first and only glimpse of an evanescent Taíno, then Navarrette's *Relación* is an early glimpse of the birth of a historical relationship between *aruacas* and a colonial (then national) society that does not disappear but rather increases in significance over time. Contemporary Lokono Arawaks, the historical descendants of the *aruacas* in Guyana, are keenly aware of their historical legacies, and it transpires that even the Taíno never completely disappeared (see discussion below). Nonetheless, the encounter with Europe was a fundamental disjuncture in native patterns of historical development, and it is the nature of that disjuncture and the new historical trajectories born of that encounter that are reflected in all the materials collected here. Navarrette's account is of particular importance for the light it sheds on the Lokono and their political and cosmological world. It is far briefer than Pané's account and, as we are told, written by someone who had never visited those lands. Their inhabitants, however, who had long been supplying food to Margarita, had constantly visited and lived with him. As the hub of the Spanish presence in the region, Margarita had manifest impacts on the native polities as far south as the province of the *aruacas* (Lokono). Current archaeological research suggests that the Berbice River, mentioned by Navarrete as the heartland of the province, was the location of dense urban-scale populations with vast systems of agricultural fields

---

19. Aside from the stand-alone editions by J. J. Arrom in Spanish (Pané 1988; a revised and expanded version of the 1974 edition) and English (1999), and those versions incorporated into various Spanish and English editions of Ferdinand Columbus's work, redacted versions of the *Antiquities* also appear in Churchill (1704), Pinkerton (1814), and Bourne (1904).

that would have been directly responsible for the *aruacas'* ability to deliver upwards of fifty tons of manioc flour in a single month.

Navarrete stresses that the *aruacas* wished to have contacts with the "Christians" and that they highly valued a political, economic, and military alliance with the Spanish. The state of constant war between *aruacas* and *caribes* reported at the opening of his account signals the significance of such an alliance, which is given a further subtle twist when Navarrete suggests that the *aruacas* were themselves in the process of driving out the *caribes*, who were the former rulers of the region. Navarrete notes that great war fleets of *aruacas* were gathered each summer to raid the *caribes*, underscoring their military capability in contrast to other *guatiaos*. His discussion of warfare and prisoners taken in battle is also a rhetorical opportunity to reinscribe the motif of cannibalistic *caribes*, who transculturate their prisoners spiritually through anthropophagic sacrifice, as opposed to the civilizing *aruacas*, who do so socially through enslavement.

Although Navarrete gives only a crude indication of *aruaca* cosmology, in contrast to Pané's rich if opaque account of Taíno ritual and mythology, one interesting detail that does emerge is the impressiveness of their astronomical knowledge. In addition, Navarrete says that an academy of teachers and prophets, the *Cemetu* (*semitci* in modern Lokono), was organized to perpetuate social and cultural memory through the formal performance of histories and their inculcation into the youth in special buildings, or "seminaries" as Navarrete calls them.

Although the *Journal* and *Letter* of Columbus, as well as the deposition of Rodrigo Figueroa and the *Relación* of Rodrigo de Navarrete, are all of special interest, it is Ramón Pané's *Antiquities* that is the most remarkable among the texts of conquest. Commissioned by Christopher Columbus in 1494, it represents the first systematic attempt to describe a culture of the Americas. Like Chanca, Pané traveled to the New World on Columbus's second voyage. He resided first on the north coast of the island of Aiti (Hispaniola) in the province of King Mayobanex and then, in early 1495, moved south to the province of King Guarionex, where he lived for nearly two years. Despite the brevity of the resulting account—about eight thousand words—it is of singular significance to historians and anthropologists of the Caribbean, not just for its ethnographic descriptions of the natives of Aiti, but also for the way in which its many linguistic and textual transformations through the centuries have made it a continuing vehicle for historiographical and ethnological debate. The often bewildering process through which Pané's text survived is discussed more below, but it is not difficult to see why it should have remained a matter of controversy, given how confusing, if not incoherent, it is. The *Antiquities* is also an unfinished manuscript, even in its first published form. Added to this is the fact that although it is an attempt at systematic ethnographic representation, it is somewhat enigmatic in its choice of ethnological subject matter. However, the title does tell us much about how Pané conceived of his task, for it is the "antiquity" of the natives that is under implicit comparison with the "modernity" of the conquerors. His very presence in the scenes that he records signals that they belong to a past that is now finished for the peoples of America, supplanted by the future that he represents.

The *Antiquities* opens with a description of the cosmology of the first beings of the native world, the wanderings of the culture hero Guagugiona, and the creation of women by men. Pané goes on to describe the use of ritual drugs, a cult of idol worship, the vision quest of shamans, and their necromancy, from which vodou may have learned the famed art of zombi making. He also relates information on native attitudes to the Spanish and the prospects for their conversion. Pané himself was certainly aware of the often haphazard nature of his account, which he relates to the character of his informants. In chapter V Pané tells us that "they are not consistent in what they say; nor it is possible to write in an orderly way what they tell." Even so, apart from this native "inconsistency," which is perhaps better understood as evidence of cultural variation, Pané creditably acknowledges in the first chapter his own omissions as an ethnographic observer: "Those I am writing about are of the island Hispaniola; that means that I do not know anything of the other islands, since I have never seen them." He does so again in chapter V: "And since they have neither letters nor writings, they do not know how to tell these stories well, nor can I write them well. Hence I believe that I will put first what should be last, and will put what is last first. But all that I write in this way is narrated by them just as I write it, and thus I note it down as I heard it from the peoples of the country." Certainly this admission makes Pané's text problematic from the point of view of contemporary anthropology, but there were also questions as to his linguistic competency in his own time: "This Fray Ramón Pané found out what he could, insofar as he understood the languages. For there were three spoken on this island: he knew only one, however, that of a small province . . . called lower Macorix; and he knew that language only imperfectly. Of the universal language he knew very little, like the rest of the Spaniards, although more than others because no-one . . . knew any of them perfectly except for a sailor . . . called Cristóbal Rodríguez" (Las Casas 1909, bk. 3, chap. 120). Las Casas adds that "all of this Fray Ramón says he has understood from the Indians. He says some other things that are confused and of little substance, as a simple person who did not speak our Castilian tongue altogether well, since he was a Catalan by birth" (chap. 167). Thus, we can never be quite sure if the confusions and apparent contradictions of the text stem from Pané's poor grasp of the indigenous language or his lack of facility with Castilian.[20] Further compounding this situation is that his account survives only as a translation into Italian, so the possible shortcomings of the translator, Alfonso de Ulloa, have to be considered as well. However, there are some more positive considerations in evaluating Pané as an ethnographer. In particular, his length of residence in Hispaniola, especially the years he spent in the province of King Guarionex, described in chapter XXV, suggest that whatever his linguistic capacities, he had the opportunity to observe much of daily life and the ritual practices of the ruling families.

Ramón Pané, as a member of the Hieronymite Order,[21] was a hermit, as he states in the opening sentence of his *Antiquities*, and this may well have suited him for the ethnographic endeavor with which Columbus had charged him. Like hermits, ethnographers consciously remove themselves from the cultural context of "normal" life in order to gain a particular kind of knowledge. A hermit, of course, will live with no social contacts whatsoever, but the limited nature of

20. However, it should be noted that Las Casas clearly plagiarized Pané's account of the ritual use of the drug *digo*, as did Martyr (see Las Casas 1909, chap. 167; Martyr 1530, dec. 1, chap. 9).

21. The writer Marina Warner (2002) suggests a link between Pané's descriptions and the work of Hieronymus Bosch, especially evident in the triptych *The Garden of Earthly Delights* (ca. 1504). In particular, Warner suggests that the accounts of the origin of women and the transformation of the dead into fruit are strongly manifested in Bosch's work (65–69). Bosch, through his Spanish patrons, may have heard about Pané's account, or even read a manuscript of it (see Warner 2002, 70).

social contact in a strange culture, the isolation of not speaking the language everyone else speaks, and the physical rigors of unfamiliar diet, climate, and customs at least suggest that one already prepared spiritually for a hermit's life may well have fared better than others.

It is also significant that the *Antiquities* was titled in Spanish as a *Relación* (deposition), which was a legal form of documentation, like the one made by Rodrigo de Figueroa.[22] Although many subsequent versions and reproductions of Pané's account use this loaded term, it is not possible to say how much Pané or his sponsor Columbus might have meant by it. But it does allow us, rather than blaming the failings of its creator, to appreciate better why the text came to have the form it does, and why what we might see as fatal flaws are in part due to the legal and political role the document came to play. Editing in any way a legally notarized deposition was no less of a suspect practice then than it is today. Paradoxically, the original is now only known through its simulacra, the first of which was the basis for the translation here, and which itself was produced in pursuit of a legal case by Ferdinand Columbus.

Despite its limitations, Ramón Pané's *Antiquities* remains the first and only extended description of the myths, rituals, and cosmology of the native people on Hispaniola; those made by Bartolomé de Las Casas and Peter Martyr, despite their criticisms, directly relied on Pané's efforts. Moreover, since the *Antiquities* was personally commissioned by Christopher Columbus, it is infused with the aura of that name. Indeed, this close association of the *Antiquities* with the tribulations of the Columbus family is directly relevant to understanding the form in which the manuscript was published. The *Antiquities* has survived only in an Italian translation made in 1571 by Alfonso de Ulloa, appearing in chapter 62 of Ferdinand Columbus's *A Life of the Admiral*. This version of Pané's text was incorporated wholesale into Ferdinand Columbus's biographical apology

22. This title implied that the account should follow certain legal requirements. First, and obviously enough, it should be a "true" account, a direct kind of reporting. This consideration is relevant when evaluating the apparent inconsistencies of the account (as discussed above). Although such inconsistencies mar an ethnography, since resolving them in informant testimony or one's own observations is the reason for the extended time that fieldwork demands, they are inevitably part of an attempt to report directly and with minimal interpretation. Moreover, the implication of the formal title *Relación* would also have been that it was reproduced without having been amended or changed in any way, being a legal testimony rather than an authorial creation.

for his father, which accompanied his legal efforts to regain family possessions and titles on the island of Hispaniola. The apology was too controversial to be published in Spanish; even after Ferdinand's death it appeared only in this Italian version.[23]

The *Antiquities* is a compelling and unique document of initial contact with the indigenous population of Hispaniola, which, through exposure to European diseases or flight away from the sites of Spanish settlement, had all but disappeared by the 1530s as colonization of the southern continent picked up pace. The *Antiquities* was thus by this time already a historical record of a vanished native culture.

Indeed, as remarked earlier, the fact that Pané chose the term "antiquities" to use in the title of the work implies that the indigenous culture he describes, while already anachronistic in the face of Spanish conquest, nevertheless may be useful to record. This is consistent with Pané's role as a missionary evangelist in the territory of King Guarionex. These aspects of Pané's *Antiquities* also speak to us in a very contemporary way, for they highlight the connections between the ethnological gaze and colonial desire, between the writing of ethnography and its wider cultural meaning and even policy applications.[24] The need for an ethnographic description of Hispaniola stemmed not from an abstract interest in human variety but from a pragmatic interest in the control and conversion of the native population through domination of its leaders. It is for this reason that Pané focuses so much on the cosmological and ritual practices of the Hispaniolan elite, and hardly at all on the forms of everyday life and subsistence.[25]

23. Columbus (1571, 1992) and see comments of Arrom (in Pané 1999, xiv) and Keen (in Columbus 1992, xiii–xvii).

24. The historical connection between colonialism and the kind of intimate knowledge of other cultures that ethnography can produce has recently been the subject of renewed debate in anthropology. Both the legacies of the Vietnam War and the need to find "Islamic specialists" in current wars on "terror" highlight this connection and its ethical complexities. See Frese and Harrell (2003); Goodman (2006); Lutz (2002); Robben (2005); Wakin (1994).

25. Pané's commission from Columbus to make a report on the indigenous population of Hispaniola was issued during a period of growing confrontation with indigenous leaders in the north of the island that resulted in the battle of Vega Real in March 1495. Notably, it was at this point that Columbus instructed Pané to move to the territory of King Guarionex, who emerged as the Spanish political proxy in the aftermath of the battle of Vega Real (La Maguá), which had devastated the power of the Taíno elite.

Pané's *Antiquities* was not the only example of this kind of "official ethnology." As already mentioned, subsequent to the destruction of the native population of Hispaniola, Spanish investors and adventurers began searching for other sources of labor. The slavery of black Africans, which Las Casas briefly advocated precisely as a means to salvage the indigenous population, eventually provided a solution to this colonial dilemma. Rodrigo de Figueroa was commissioned in 1518 to investigate and discriminate *caribe* populations throughout the Caribbean and coastal South America. Unrelated to the controversies of the Columbian legacy, Figueroa's report never achieved the subsequent fame of Pané's *Antiquities*, but in a similar fashion it attempted to define and locate political authority, cultural proclivity, and military ability, as a prelude to the conquest and enslavement of those populations. In place of the apparently tractable peoples depicted by Pané as a promising context for the establishment of empire,[26] Figueroa portrays the wider Caribbean and mainland as riven by a fundamental cultural dualism in which the cannibalistic and warlike *caribes* threaten to overwhelm Spain's natural allies, the *aruaca* or *guatiaos* of Hispaniola and Puerto Rico. This portrayal both licenses the legal enslavement of vast numbers of native peoples and, by allusion to the supposed depredations of the *caribes*, allows the Spanish Crown to evade moral responsibility for the destruction of the Hispaniolan natives. Thus, it is critical that we read Pané's *Antiquities* not as an isolated and idiosyncratic work, but rather as a text with a political and cultural background to both its production and dissemination.

The nature of its transmission requires that we critically assess how the *Antiquities* functioned in the context of demonstrating Columbus family claims to Hispaniola, since it certainly seems as if Ferdinand was intent on marshaling any and all evidence he could for that purpose. The inclusion of this unfinished and often incoherent text in the *Life of the Admiral* may in turn stem from the way in which that work was hastily fashioned from the legal materials collected for the Columbus family's legal dispute with the Crown. Ferdinand's hobby as a collector of books and manuscripts might

---

26. It should be stressed that in fact native armies were militarily significant, numbering tens of thousands of warriors; as in the later conquest of Mexico, they were defeated through a combination of political strategy and elaborate military technology.

have led to a catch-all approach to this task, and, as Ferdinand himself notes, Pané's *Antiquities* "contains so many fictions that the only sure thing to be learned from it is that the Indians have a certain natural reverence for the after-life and believe in the immortality of the soul" (1992, 153). However, this judgment is misplaced for many reasons, not least because the now-lost Spanish manuscript was also a source for Las Casas's accounts of the indigenous population in the *Apologética historia* (chaps. 120, 166–67) and Peter Martyr's descriptions of the peoples of Hispaniola in *De orbo novo decades* (1516, dec. 1, chap. 9). The *Antiquities'* survival and transmission in various forms occurred not just because of its potential value as an ethnological description, but also because it directly underpins a positive evaluation of the reputation of Christopher Columbus through its allusion to a pristine, almost innocent, moment of encounter between Spain and the Indies, before subsequent colonial despoilers destroyed the natives of Hispaniola.[27] In this way, one may come to see its lapses as a product of this context of production, not simply the ethnographic shortcomings of Pané himself, even if these remain a relevant consideration.

Challenging the linguistic competence of Ramón Pané has been one of the major forms of critique of his account, and to some extent the *Antiquities* invites this approach since it is full of, even overloaded with, Pané's versions of native terms.[28] At the same time, the *Antiquities'* iconic status as a record of vanished culture entails that the interpretation and usage of those native terms given by Pané, or later variants based on them, have a complex and even politically charged history.[29] For example, the term *Taíno*, which is currently in

27. But see Samuel Wilson's (1990) careful account of the conquest of Hispaniola in the closing years of the fifteenth century.

28. This should not imply a need to clean up or make uniform Pané's own inconsistent spellings. For example, in the Italian text of the *Antiquities* the name of the legendary hero "Guagugiona" is also rendered as "Giocauugama" and "Guaguiona." Even if Pané was unable to account for them, these orthographic differences may reflect ritual ones, and thus erasing them means that for scholarly purposes information may be lost. Therefore, in this edition all terms are given as they appear in the Italian translation of Pané's lost original.

29. Arrom (1988, but starting in the original 1974 edition) took up the linguistic and etymological debate that had been initiated by E. G. Bourne's (1906) translation and annotation of Pané. Arrom clearly demonstrated the fallacy of a number of Bourne's interpretations and provided new identifications and interpretations of names and words found in Pané's *Antiquities*. This was an important and invaluable exercise,

vogue to refer to the indigenous population of the western Antilles, centering on Hispaniola, is a purely nineteenth-century invention by the antiquarian C. S. Rafinesque.[30] It derives from the phrase, recorded in the early Spanish documentation, *ni-taino*, meaning "my-lord." There is no evidence that this phrase was ever used by native people to designate the ethnic identity of themselves or others, and it does not appear in Pané's writings. Apparently unnoticed by previous commentators on the *Antiquities*, perhaps due to an exclusive focus on these linguistic and etymological issues, is that Pané quite clearly states in chapter V, "Hispaniola, which before was called Aiti, and *that is how its inhabitants are called* [my emphasis]; and that one and other islands are called Bouhi." The term *guatiao*, which has evident phonetic connections with both these native terms, *Aiti* and *Bouhi*, was generically used to indicate allies or partners and thus describes culturally similar or nonthreatening groups, with the term *caribe* designating enemies or strangers. As discussed previously, following Figueroa's report the term *aruaca*, deriving from the name given to native allies of the Spanish colonists on the northern Venezuelan coast, becomes more prevalent than *guatiao*, signaling the erasure of the indigenous political systems of Hispaniola and the growing importance of the possibilities for alliance and trade with the vast continent of South America. The key point, then, is that such terms were sociopolitical, not ethnolinguistic, in their reference, as was evident in the discussion of Figueroa's report above. In that case, we must appreciate that modern usage of these terms—*caribe*,

---

but Arrom chose a distinct methodology: to try and reconstruct and make systematic the lost original Spanish manuscript of Pané. This project originates with the nineteenth-century Cuban intellectual Antonio Bachiller y Morales and has become entwined with the laudable ambitions of Antilleanist scholars to give due weight and significance to the Amerindian heritage of the Caribbean through a serious scholarly attempt to reconstitute its cultural and linguistic forms. However, this project also has its limitations from the perspective of historical anthropology since it is apt to lead to the erasure of possibly significant information (see previous note). This is the case, for example, in Arrom's resolution of the terminological ambiguities in the orthography of the term *naboria* or servant, as recorded in other early sources about Hispaniola. Arguably, the term *giahuuauariù*, as given in chapter 25 of the Italian translation of Pané's *Antiquities*, is actually cognate with *inharou/oubéerou*, native terms for a female concubine, suggesting a gendered as well as rank coding of social status between rulers and their subject populations.

30. See note 15.

guatiao, aruaca, Taíno—still bears the weight of past and continuing controversy.

The persistence of such disputes is partly due to the orthography in Pané's *Antiquities*, which is so intricate as almost to defy interpretation and which therefore has been the source of many dubious etymologies. Pané transcribed the speech acts of indigenous people over five hundred years ago, not into his natal tongue (Catalan) but into Castilian Spanish. This Spanish version was then translated into Italian for inclusion in a Venetian publication of Ferdinand Columbus's biography of his father, and the original was lost. All subsequent Spanish editions are therefore themselves translations from Italian, as is the newly translated English-language version presented here. The plethora of native words and names, far richer than in any other contemporary, and many later, accounts, is a key feature of Pané's *Antiquities*. To this day, all the word lists of a supposed Taíno language ultimately derive from Ramón Pané's transcription of over one hundred terms. As a result, much of the scholarship surrounding the *Antiquities* has focused almost exclusively on making sense of this orthography and its many transformations since 1494. The first English translation, based on the Italian version of Ferdinand Columbus's work, was made by Edward Gaylord Bourne in 1906, and the only current English-language edition is José Juan Arrom's version, translated by Susan Griswold, of his 1988 Spanish edition.[31] Thus, no direct translation of the Italian into English has been made for over a century.

Both archaeologists and ethnohistorians, as well as Antilleanist intellectuals, uncritically adopted the term *Taíno*, overlooking Pané's clear statement that the proper term was *Aiti*, and in doing so continued the inventive process begun by Rafinesque in the nineteenth

31. Arrom's Spanish text is actually a mix of the Italian translation made by Ulloa, the "epitome" made by Peter Martyr D'Anghera in *De orbe nouo* (1530/1912), and the descriptions given by Las Casas in *Apologetica historia* (1909). Arrom chose this procedure as a response to the shortcomings he perceived in Pané's linguistic and literary abilities, and with the presumption that the materials from Martyr and Las Casas should be given ethnological and linguistic priority over Pané's own descriptions. While the text is consequently far more accessible, it is a bowdlerized version that is useless for the purposes of scholarly study since it begs those very questions that Pané's writings might otherwise be used to answer. See also chapt. 3, note 51. Also notable is that Martyr, unlike Las Casas, never went to the Indies, much less Hispaniola.

century. As we shall see, this has also had an impact on issues of contemporary cultural resistance and survival throughout the Caribbean. However, the field of anthropological and historical linguistics recently has undergone a shift in theoretical perspectives, such that the basic language classifications of twenty years ago are no longer universally accepted as valid. Instead they are often seen as descriptive of little else than the word lists that were used to construct them. There is now a far greater interest in the careful discrimination of historical speech communities, rather than formal linguistic structures. This change results from the recognition of the linguistic plurality of many Amerindian cultures, not least those on Hispaniola, as Pané's *Antiquities* makes perfectly clear. At the same time, the complex nature of the publication and translations of Pané's *Antiquities* means that the orthographic analogies by which many have attempted to reconstruct a Taíno language are at best only suggestive, and at worst actually misleading. The hypothetical etymologies that are employed to demonstrate continuities or shared properties with ethnographically recorded languages can therefore create the impression of a speech community that never in fact existed. In the context of Pané's description of the linguistic situation on Hispaniola in chapter XXV of his work, for example, the differences in speech he notes could have been related to social and political rank or even gender as much as ethnic identity.[32]

This view of linguistic practice and plurality also has profound implications for a notion of unitary Taíno culture, which in turn has importance for Antilleanist intellectuals and for still-surviving indigenous populations of the Antilles. But this importance is a distinct issue from that of the historical and ethnological accuracy of using this term for designating past indigenous populations. A quite considerable historical and anthropological literature has developed in the last few years concerning both the native population of the Caribbean and the history of native society and culture in South America

---

32. It is well established that the *caribe* populations of the Antilles employed both a natal Arawakan language and, among men, a Cariban-based pidgin called Kalinago (Breton 1665, 1666). How this situation arose has been the subject of prolonged debate, but the point here is that the origins of linguistic differences cannot be treated as uniform across all contexts. A failure to recognize this fundamental principle of sociolinguistics has marred discussion of linguistic practices on Hispaniola (see Whitehead 1995).

more generally.[33] These new analyses and the kinds of data on which they are based might now be fruitfully used for a broader reading of Pané's *Antiquities* and its implicit understandings, as well as the more overt ethnological items with which earlier editions chiefly deal. Moreover, consonant with the current tendency by anthropologists to emphasize individual agency within social and cultural structures, as well as the symbiotic and mimetic nature of social and cultural interchange in the course of colonial encounter, much more can be inferred as to the nature of Pané's ethnographic experience, its wider implications for a reading of his *Antiquities,* and the context of other contemporary ethnological writings. Thus, the significance of the materials Pané presents, the forms of representation he chooses, and the argumentation by which they are interpreted necessarily become integral to the textual commentary.

Pané himself certainly shows an admirable degree of that reflexivity and awareness as to how observation is born of expectation as much as experience—a consideration that ethnographers now consider indispensable to their own writings on distant peoples. In point of fact, Pané is ethnographically reflexive on precisely the issue of his lack of a systematic portrayal of native culture, as he is no less frank about missing information that he failed to collect. In this way the text itself may be said to implicitly illustrate the context for Pané's ethnography. Through a close reading of his *Antiquities* we also may be able to perceive some of the nuances of the varying political interests and ritual proclivities of the native population. This is particularly so in the passages in chapters XV and XVI that discuss the conversion of King Guarionex. Equally in need of further interpretation and commentary are the descriptions of the *cimi* (also rendered as *zemi* in subsequent literature) cult and its attendant ritual, since earlier editions discuss only the putative etymologies and translations of the names of *cimis.* But the superfluity of names that Pané displays was perhaps designed as much to give his work an ethnographic authority as it was to provide systematic cultural information. The persistent iteration of exotic names thus can be understood as compensating for the other ethnographic "inadequacies" of the text itself. In any case, not all names have a literal meaning, but

33. See Whitehead (1992, 1995, 1999a, 1999b, 2002a), Ralegh (1997), and associated bibliographic discussions.

they are unique descriptors and so need not be considered correct or incorrect.

That earlier emphasis on the cultural significance of the etymology and meaning of *cimi* names generally precludes consideration of other aspects of the descriptions in Pané's *Antiquities* that contemporary historical anthropologists would consider central, such as the elite nature of *cimi* worship, or the prophecy of the Spaniards' arrival by the *cimi* Giocauugama, recounted in chapter XV:

> They say that this *cacique* claimed that he had talked with Giocauugama, who told him that those who would have survived him would enjoy their rule for a short time, because dressed people would arrive in their country, who would dominate and kill them, and that they would starve to death. At first they thought that these people had to be the *cannibali*, but then they considered that since they [the *cannibali*] do not do anything else other than grab and run, it had to be other people that the *cimi* indicated. Hence, they now believe that these are the admiral and the people that he brings.

The identification of the Spanish with the "cannibal *caribes*" is notable in this passage and ironically reflects the actual outcome of the arrival of the "dressed people," who did indeed utterly consume the population of Hispaniola. The relative scarcity, which Las Casas emphasizes (1909, 65ff), of *cimi* worship outside Hispaniola also seems to directly contradict the idea often inferred by commentators on the *Antiquities* of a unitary, or even very widespread, Taíno culture. Moreover, both Las Casas and particularly Pané indicate that their observations relate rather more to the practices of the rulers than the ruled. Pané writes in chapter XIII, "I have seen parts of this with my own eyes, while of the other things I narrated only what I learned from many, especially the principal men, with whom I practiced more than with others; since they believe these tales more certainly than the others." In short, the nature of Ramón Pané's text can be better revealed through a direct historical ethnography of the Taíno themselves, in addition to the kinds of textual commentary and lexical analysis that have otherwise constituted the main forms of critique.

Cosmology and Ritual in the Taíno World

As is inevitable in any ethnographic enterprise, Pané's interests and opportunities were skewed by the social context of his informants. But because his informants were mostly the lords and kings of the provinces he resided in as a guest of Kings Mayobanex and Guarionex, his account gives us significant insight into the cosmology of the indigenous population, particularly the foundational myths of creation and the establishment of political authority and order, topics that would have been of particular relevance for the ruling elite. What kind of "guest" Pané may have been and how his hosts understood his residency cannot be properly reconstructed, but this context certainly commands close attention to the results of that sojourn. Lacking historical background and uninformative as to the wider networks of indigenous political life, Pané's information is only a snapshot of the indigenous world on Aiti.[34]

Central to this mythic charter for the Taíno political order were the myth-histories of the heroes and divinities Guagugiona and Caracaracol, introduced in chapters IV and X, respectively: "Guagugiona left with the women and went looking for other lands, and he arrived at Matinino, where he immediately left the women, and went to another region called Guanin, and they had left the small children by a creek." This brief passage, with the benefit of wider reading in Pané's own text as well as other contemporary sources and subsequent accounts and ethnographies, summates a key principle in the charter. Thus, the first ancestor, Guagugiona, when he left Aiti for Matinino (Martinique), persuaded the women to accompany him, abandoning their husbands but bringing with them their children and a cargo of the drug *digo*; at Matinino they saw beautiful seashells (*cobo*), which, following the example of Guagugiona's brother-in-law, they descended into the sea to admire. Here they were left by Guagugiona, who then returned with the first *guanin* (gold-copper-alloy

---

34. As a result, Stevens-Arroyo (1998, 3–17) adopts an explicitly structuralist approach to interpreting these materials, analyzing the internal structures of the myths and rituals in the attempt to reveal the underlying "mytho-logic" through which indigenous thought approached those perennial human questions of birth, copulation, and death.

objects) and *ciba* (magic stones, also called *takua*).[35] In this context the term "caribe" therefore seems to allude to a political, not an ethnic, status, deriving from the mythology of Guagugiona as originator of a political and economic order in which persons are exchanged for things (gold and jade work) with groups living in the southern Antillean islands and the continent. The myth cycle establishes the ideological underpinning of an elite trade in which drugs, seashells (shell necklaces), and persons (women and children) were exchanged for gold and magic stones (*takua*), the latter significantly being carved mostly in the form of frogs. Matinino, "the island of women," represents the site of these exchanges, replicating the pattern of exchange that Spanish sources coded as *caribe* aggression against the people of Aiti (see also Oliver 2009, 157). The connection of Matinino with the Amazon-women myth cycle of the South American continent is reinforced by the origin of the *ciba* as derived from female water spirits, just as the continental *takua* were said to be made by the "water mama," who to this day still supplies the stones for smoothing pottery among the Pomeroon Karinya of coastal Guyana, called *caribes* in Spanish sources. In this symbolic and mythic context, it is not difficult to see why the *caribes* of Martinique, Dominica, and Guadeloupe, as a result of their intimate connections of war, marriage, and trade with the people of Aiti, were constructed as consumers of persons, or "cannibals."[36] In this context, it also becomes possible to understand the otherwise contradictory observation that Caonabó, one of the other principal caciques of Aiti, was himself a *caribe* according to contemporary sources. This again underlines the point that *caribe* was a political, as much as cultural or ethnic, designation (see also Oliver 2009, xv).

Given, then, the importance of establishing elite male predominance in the system of extra-island exchanges, the myth of the *caracaracol* men, and in particular the figure of Dimiuan Caracaracol,

35. In Pané's version, the children were simply abandoned in a ditch on Martinique. Martyr says they were turned into frogs.

36. For example, in Chanca's description of Guadeloupe (Gil and Varela 1984, 158–59) it is clear that cotton work was a major item of production; in his opinion the cloaks rivaled those of Spain. It is in this context that we are also informed about the captive women who were held here; it seems plausible to suggest that the use of such women for the *caribes* was primarily as producers of such items, not as victims for a cannibal feast; just as, for example, on the mainland they were critical to the production of dye and, as processors of manioc, were key to the political ambitions of men.

inscribes male action as also at the source of gender differentiation. Pané writes in chapter VII

> that one day men went washing themselves; . . . they were longing to have some women, . . . without being able to find any news of them, but that day . . . they saw coming down from some trees, lowering down along the branches, a certain shape of person, which were neither men nor women, neither had they masculine or feminine characteristics; which they went to capture; but they escaped, as if they were eels. . . . They called two or three men . . . to go and . . . seek out for each one of them a *caracaracol* man, because they have coarse hands; so they could hold them tight. . . . And so they brought in four *caracaracoli* men; said *caracaracoli* is a disease, like scabies, that makes the body very coarse. After they caught them, they deliberated on how to make them women, since they had neither a male nor female nature.

This the men did: "They went looking for a bird called *inriri* . . . that makes holes in the trees [woodpecker]. Likewise, they took those women with neither male nor female nature, and tied their hands and feet, and got the aforesaid bird, and tied it to their body, and thinking they were wood beams it started its usual work, pecking and puncturing in the place where it usually happens that the nature of women is. In this way, then, the Indians say they got women, according to what the elders tell." Pané follows this account with another disclaimer: "Given that I wrote quickly, and I that did not have enough paper, I could not put in the right place what by mistake I moved to another place. But with all this I am not mistaken, because they believe everything as it is written. Let us now return to what we should have put first, namely their opinion on the origin and beginning of the sea." Pané goes on to relate how, from a monstrous swelling on his back (clearly depicted in figure 1), one of the *caracaracol* men, Dimiuan, gives birth to a turtle, first creature of the sea, with the help of his "nameless" brothers. The men thus make women with a woodpecker, and then, in an act of ancestral cannibalism, Dimiuan Caracaracol, by eating the first children of these women, establishes the right of men to consume the progeny of women as wives and slaves. Caught in the act, Dimiuan drops a gourd of water and causes the Caribbean Sea to flow into the world. In these mythic realms, then, men, especially lordly men, are constructed as originators of sociality, its inverse cannibalism, and the geographical landscape of the islands (see map 1).[37]

Apart from these charters of social origin and masculine control, Pané gives many details and insights into the ritual means through which this order was sustained. In particular, the *cimis* (which he also calls *cimini* or *cimiches*) were powerful idols of stone, wood, or other plant materials that were kept in the possession of the *caciques* (see figs. 4–6). The text of the *Antiquities* gives many details about the *cimis'* names, proclivities, origins, and so forth.[38] Pané nicely summarizes their variety in chapter XV: "The majority of those of the island of Hispaniola have many *cimini* of various kinds. Some hold the bones of the father, or of the mother, or of the relatives, or of the forebears; and they are made of stone or wood. And of the two kinds they have many: some that speak, others that make food grow, others that make rain, and others that make winds blow." It is clear from the text of the *Antiquities* that such *cimi* were only contingently realized in these material forms and were a class of spirits that, as in other shamanic complexes in this region, could also be used and dialogued with through the ritual performance of the *bohuti* (also called *buhuitihu* in the text). In chapter XXIV Pané gives a very important description of this dialogue and the materialization of the *cimi* spirit through the making of carved idols. A shaman addresses a tree that has been seen to move its roots: " 'Tell me who you are, and what you are doing here, and what you want from

---

37. Clearly such themes and interpretations are established through a wider corpus of materials, extending beyond the writings of Pané. Stevens-Arroyo (1988) in particular has done much to reveal a deeper vision of the aboriginal cosmos and social order. The point here is that Pané's writings are fundamental to any such project and consistent, in ways not apparent to either Pané or some of his later detractors, with materials relating to the Caribbean before 1492.

38. Figure 1 is a funerary *cimi* that X-ray examination has shown holds human remains. Figure 4 is a *cimi* of stone thought to have been buried for fertility reasons. This example also shows the rounded eyes and grimace associated with Machetaurie. Figure 5 shows Opigielguouiran, of whom Pané records, "they say that has four legs like a dog, and it is made of wood, and at night it often went outside into the forest. They would seek it, and take it back home, and tie it with ropes, but it would go back to the forest. And they say that when the Christians arrived in the island Hispaniola, it fled and went in a lagoon, and they followed its tracks there; but they do not see it anymore, and know nothing of it. As I bought it, I am selling it" (*Antiquities* chap. 22).

me, and why you sent for me. Tell me if you want that I cut you, or if you want to come with me, and how do you want that I carry you, and I will build you a house with possessions.' So that tree, or *cimiche*, made idol, or devil, answers, telling him the form in which he wants to be made. And he cuts it, and makes it in the way he ordered him."

One dramatic aspect of the ritual performance of the *bohuti* described by Pané that has hitherto been completely ignored concerns necromancy. Haiti has become notorious for the practice of vodou, and particularly the creation of zombis, or resurrection of the dead. Although it is usually thought to have derived exclusively from African practices brought by the black slaves, there are a number of reasons, beginning with Pané's text, to suppose that in fact this aspect of vodou necromancy was also strongly informed by contacts with the still-surviving aboriginal population of the island. Just as the name Haiti obviously derives from the native name Aiti, so too do aspects of the zombi ritual derive from vodou. Moreover, the term *zombi* is no less plausibly derived from the cognate word recorded by Pané as *cimini* and in other Caribbean languages, such as Karipuna, as *cimi* or *zemi*, where also the suffix -*iba* designates the material and fleshly form that spirit beings might adopt. *Zemi-iba* (spirit of flesh) seems no less likely as the source for this term than the current derivation in Africanist scholarship from the name of a West African deity, one not even associated with resurrection or death cults. Of course, to follow this line of reasoning is to risk committing the same error of etymological obsession that has previously so limited the interpretations made from Pané's text. It is the startling description of zombi making in chapter XVII of Pané's text that is the real evidence here:

They take the juice of the leaves and cut the nails and the hair bangs of the dead and they pulverize them with two stones and mix them with the juice of the said herb, and they give it to the dead to drink by the nose or the mouth; and while they do this they ask the dead person if the doctor [*bohuti*] was the cause of his death. . . . And they ask this several times, *until the dead person speaks as if he were alive; in a such way he answers all that they want to know from him,* saying that the *buhuitihu* did not follow the diet, or on that occasion was responsible of his death; and they say that the doctor asks him if he is alive, and how it is that he speaks so clearly; and he answers that he is dead. And having known what they wanted to know, they return him to the grave, from where they took him, to know from him what we just said.

If this were just an isolated report of shamanic resurrection of the dead, it would still have an important bearing on understanding the origins of vodou. But in fact the ability to kill and resurrect is a defining skill of the shaman throughout South America (Whitehead 2002b; Whitehead and Wright 2004). In my ethnographic account of *kanaimà* (dark shamans) among the Patamuna of Guyana, the power of resurrection, *wulukatok* in the Patamuna language, is central to shamanic power. As I was told by one informant, "My father was so Amerindian. . . . He no went school, and he could kill and resurrect you in a day!" (Whitehead 2002b, 174). Obviously this is not to deny African influence in magic of zombi making, but it is relevant to note that the zombi maker in Haitian vodou is called the *bokor*, not the *houngan:* while the *houngan* is a priest and associated with genealogy, family magic, and curing, the *bokor* is an outsider figure, possibly due to the derivation of this role from indigenous shamanic practices.[39] Within Haitian vodou, zombi making is connected with the Bizango ceremony of the Petwa rite, and Baron Samedi, its principal deity, was actually "born" in America, according to vodou practitioners. The Bizango rite itself stems from the earliest slave transportations from Senegal-Gambia, and rebel communities of such slaves, together with refugee indigenes, are clearly recorded on Aiti from the early sixteenth century onwards. This was the fertile context for a melding of African and American shamanic forms, and there were many contacts, even after the supposed disappearance of

39. As a term, *bokor* seems related to *bohuti* as given in Pané. But there are other terms to which *bokor* might also relate, all meaning "spirit master" in indigenous vocabularies of the islands, such *boye, boyaicu,* and *niboyei* (see Breton 1665). Current suggestions that the word "zombi" comes from an Angolan deity named Nzambi are derived from the poet Robert Southey (1819, 3:24) in his nineteenth-century *History of Brazil.* However, this deity, unlike the *bokor* and rituals of zombi making, is firmly associated with positive spiritual value. So it seems no less likely that the origin was connected to the cemi of the Caribbean. Indeed, Pané also tells us that the name for the malevolent dead was *opia,* which relates to the non-Haitian term for dark shamanism, *obeah* (Apter 2002; Beauvoir-Dominique 1995).

the indigenous population, between rebel slaves and remnant native groups. The intellectual trend to derive vodou from West Africa comes much later, following the French occupation of Aiti, so it is relevant to note that "Haiti" was the name given by Henri Christophe and the other slave rebels to their new black republic at the end of the eighteenth century. A legacy of war magic and dark shamanism among escaped slaves, stemming from Amerindian modes of spirituality, is also signaled by the fact that the rite that initiated the great slave uprising against the French was the Bwa Kayiman ritual, dedicated to the lord of the forests, realm of the Amerindians.

The wider context for Caribbean necromancy is not only Amazonian shamanism but also of course the Aztec and their Lord of Night and Sorcery, Tezcatlipoca, whose skull-like face is a recurrent motif in ceremonial objects from Cuba, Haiti, Puerto Rico, and the Dominican Republic. Even more apparent is the similarity in depictions of the Aztec Lord of the Dead, Mictlantecuhtli, and in representations on *cohoba* equipment (fig. 2) and *cimis* (fig. 5), possibly of Machetaurie, Lord of the House of the Dead, mentioned in chapter XII of the *Antiquities*. Likewise, the "spectacled" figure of Tlaloc, widespread in Central American cultures, is suggested in Caribbean ceremonial objects that have abnormally rounded and outlined eyes (ethnographically associated with shamanic vision), especially on masks, which were a prominent part of Central American as well as Caribbean ceremonial equipment. Indeed, a mask with such "spectacles," as well as other eyepieces made from shell, are all reported archaeologically as well as in contemporary descriptions.[40]

It is no less suggestive, then, that *Dumbala*—a snake spirit in vodou—may also be related to indigenous practice in the way in which the *bohuti* could be resurrected even after being killed and dismembered, specifically by being licked on the face by a swarm of many differently colored snakes commanded by the *bohuti*, as described in chapter XVIII:

> At night they say that many snakes of various kinds come, white, black, and green, and of many other colors, which lick the face and the whole body of the aforesaid doctor, who, as we

40. Baron Samedi, lord of crossroads and graveyards, and so also of resurrection and zombis, is spectacled in this way, except that the sunglasses he wears are always missing the right lens.

said, was thought dead and left there; and he stays there two or three nights; and they say that while he stays there, the bones of the legs and arms join again and heal, and that he stands up and walks slowly and goes back home; and those who see him question him, saying, "Were you not dead?" but he answers that the *cimini* came to help him in the form of snakes.

The exercise of such dramatic and profound spiritual power was also connected to the ruling *caciques* through the *cohoba* cult. Pané comments on the cult just once, in chapter XV, speaking about the *bohuti:* "To purge himself he takes a certain powder called *cohoba,* inhaling it by the nose, which intoxicates him in such a way that they do not know what they do; and they say many things out of the ordinary, in which they affirm that they talk with the *cimini,* and that they tell them that the illness came from them." However, the archaeological artifact assembly and other historical accounts, such as that of Las Casas, all suggest that this was an activity not just of the *bohuti* but of the *caciques* as well. Pané's relative silence on this ritual may be related to his general emphasis on cosmology and spiritual practice rather than the sphere of political order. By the same token, Pané does not mention ball courts or the *duho* (ceremonial throne) at all, yet these items of material culture, as well as the ritual equipment for the *cohoba* cult of the *caciques,* consisting of elaborately decorated trays, pestles, mortars, and vomit spatulas (see fig. 3), are among the key material remains of native culture in the Caribbean (Bercht et al. 1997).

Pané concludes the *Antiquities* with a sense of the gathering storm of destruction that woul devastate and disperse the native population of Aiti. Having recorded the prophecy of the coming of the "dressed people," he relates the following incident in chapters XXIV–XXV: "Six men went to the house of prayer, which the catechumens, who were seven, had under guard, and by order of Guarionex they told them to take the images that Fray Roman had left in custody of the aforementioned catechumens and to smash them and tear them apart. . . . As they left the house of prayer, they threw the images on the ground, and they covered them with soil and pissed on them, saying: 'Now your fruits will be good and large'; and then they buried them in a garden." Even Guarionex, who had not taken part in the first battle of Vega Real, is by this point clearly more resistant to Spanish dominance.[41] Pané's own opinion on conversion, given in chapter XXVI, makes evident enough why such resistance was growing even among those initially cooperative with the Spanish:

> Truly the island is in great need of people to punish the lords when they deserve it, make them understand the things of the saint Catholic faith, and train them in that. . . .
>
> . . . The first Christian [was] Giauauuariú, in whose house there were seventeen persons, who all became Christians, just by letting them know that there is one God, who made everything and created the sky and the earth, with nothing else being argued or explained; given that, they easily believed. But with the others force and ingenuity are necessary, because not everyone is of the same nature: therefore, if they had a good beginning and a better end, there would be others who would start well and then would laugh at what is taught to them; for them force and punishment are necessary.

So began the conquest of America.

Unending Conquest, Enduring Resistance

The primal visions in these early texts have great significance in the contemporary cultural politics of the Caribbean, as well as in the persistence of the indigenous peoples they try to describe. The tragedy of the European conquest and colonization of the Caribbean and the rest of the Americas would be hard to overstate. But in the case of the peoples of the Caribbean, this has all too often been assumed to entail their complete erasure, physically and culturally, an assumption that has suited the triumphalist historiography that often informs the "heroic" tale of a few "brave and true" Europeans dominating, against the demographic odds, the vast and populous territories of their "New World." But, as in the still-unfolding history of the *aruacas*, the figure of the all-conquering European obscures the important histories of continuity and survival of native peoples into the present

---

41. Curiously, Arrom (in Pané 1988, xxi) obscures this act of native resistance, seeing it more as the Spaniards misunderstanding an indigenous fertility ceremony.

day. Equally, exculpatory emphasis on the impersonal forces of biology and technology, important though they may have been, neglects the fact that the presence of those biologies and the deployment of those technologies were no less the product of European political decisions than the overt violence of slavery, war, and missionary conversion. Despite the virulence of the epidemics that followed the first contacts in the late fifteenth century, there were still plenty of natives against whom wars of conquest and extermination could be waged well into the late nineteenth century, as occurred in the United States. In point of fact, the peoples of Aiti did not disappear or fade away quietly but have remained a physical presence throughout the Caribbean, even if this has been unacknowledged by successive governments that preferred to assimilate such survivors into the lowest ranks of the new colonial order that emerged during the sixteenth century (Whitehead 1999a).

Political alliance and social interconnection with the *cimarrones* (rebel black slaves) who were imported to support a plantation economy, as well as migration to the smaller islands and mainland of South America, were important factors in the indigenous history of this region. Equally, the emergence of the *caribes* as both indomitable opponents and vital collaborators in the colonial design of the region encompassed refugee groups from Hispaniola and Puerto Rico. Recognition of this legacy in the idea of nationhood has occurred only recently, but Pané's text has been a vehicle for recovering the importance of native peoples for an Antilleanist historiography of the Caribbean in which, if not fully incorporated as political actors, indigenous people nonetheless loom large as necessary progenitors of Caribbean modernity. Although I have commented above on the indigenous legacies present within vodou (and the related mainland practice of obeah) only as they relate to Pané's text, such legacies within Afro-American cultures have recently begun to be more clearly recognized as a widespread component of American history.[42]

More generally, the way in which the *Antiquities* has captured the imagination of so many is reflected in its continuing relevance to the cultural revival of the Taíno nation and the establishment of the indigenist presence in modern Caribbean society. This process becomes materially and ideologically evident through the production

42. As has the historical significance of the interconnections between "blacks and reds" in the Americas more generally; see Restall (2005).

of the idea of the "Taíno" as an aesthetic commodity and as a source of political assertion. As an aesthetic commodity, the term *Taíno* and recreated images of Taíno persons circulate widely in the Caribbean, particularly in Puerto Rico and the Dominican Republic, as well as among immigrant communities in the United States.[43] More central to cultural revival has been the formation of a Taíno nation[44] with its own flag, leadership, and promotion of cultural events to re-enact and rehearse "Taíno" culture:

> We the Taíno People and Nation have been involved in the serious and difficult task of restoration and implementation of the diverse aspects of our culture and heritage.
>
> For the past 17 years our main work has been to bring the People together; reconnecting individuals and families into a People and Nation.
>
> The very concept of "being a People" itself had to be brought back.
>
> As a result of our work the myth of extinction has been shattered; Identity established and the culture and ancestral language revitalized.[45]

In this process, Pané's text has been a valuable primary source of lexical recovery and suggestions for the re-creation of cultural behavior, as with the *zemi* (*cimi*) cult. Inevitably, re-creation of the spiritual

43. Cigars, bananas, rap records, bumper stickers, Dominican ten and hundred peso notes, and a UNESCO medal all bear the image or term "Taíno."

44. Taíno groups in different islands and the mainland United States have formed separate entities such as the Jatibonicu Taino Tribal Nation of Boriken (http://members .dandy.net/~orocobix/ or http://www.taino-tribe.org/jatiboni.html) and the Jatibonicù Taino Tribal Band of New Jersey (http://www.hartford-hwp.com/Taino/jatibonuco .html), which are federally recognized Native American entities (http://www.usa .gov/Government/Tribal_Sites/J.shtml). There are also non-U.S. organizations in the Caribbean, such as the Taíno Nation of the Antilles (http://nacion_taina.tripod.com/), as well as other U.S. organizations, such as the United Confederation of Taino People (http://www.uctp.org/), offering a wide variety of information. Inevitably, there are disagreements over which organization truly represents "Taíno" heritage, but activities like a boycott of the recent Hollywood film *Pirates of the Caribbean: Dead Man's Chest* provide opportunities for unity and to associate with other indigenous groups such as the "caribes," or Caribs, of Dominica, where some of the film was shot. For the various flags of the Taíno nations, see http://www.crwflags.com/fotw/flags/xh-taino .html.

45. Statement at Taíno Nation Web site, http://members.tripod.com/nacion_taina/ id15.html).

order has been less a matter of developing shamanic technique and more an aesthetic engagement with the idea of "Taíno" and indigenous resistance to the Spanish. Heroic portraits of Taíno warriors, modern renderings of *zemi* carvings, re-enactments of Taíno ceremonies and clothing, and an interest in the preservation of archaeological sites are all expressions of this newfound nationhood. Pané's text is at one and the same time idiosyncratic, partial, credulous, and cynical, but in the end it is all that remains of that first moment of violent encounter between the Spanish war fleets and the peoples of Aiti and other islands. This structural position in the architecture of history in the Americas means that Pané's text will always overcome its shortcomings as history or anthropology and will always be closely studied and commented on, even as our interests in what it may tell us constantly change in conjunction with the shifting cultural agendas and historiographical desires of the day. In a similar way, the documents of Columbus, Chanca, Figueroa, and Navarrete collected here function to establish the counterposed ethnological and political categories of *caribe* and *aruaca* (although the much wider story that Rodrigo de Navarrete shows us, of how not only *aruacas* but also *caribes* went on to be "discovered" throughout northern South America, is beyond the scope of this volume). By the pairing of these extracts with Pané's account the emergence of these ethnological and cultural categories can be better understood, as can the political persistence of *caribes* and *aruacas*, who represent historical responses to the challenges of interacting with a growing Atlantic world. Such processes are over five hundred years old and so have produced ethnic sentiments that express these original categories of conquest. The Caribs in Dominica, Honduras, and Belize who represent the descendants of those first *caribes* thus take pride in their resistant and rebellious history and now see the charge of cannibalism as a source of grim satisfaction, not shame.[46] Of course there is a much wider story told through the documents of Columbus, Chanca, Figueroa, Pané,

---

46. For an excellent study of similar revival processes amongst "caribe" peoples of the Caribbean, see Forte (2005). Lynne Guitar (2002) has also done much to document the persistence and survival of indigenous people in the Dominican Republic, despite the "myth of Taíno extinction." Hulme and Whitehead (1992) gather together a selection of writings, including the parts of Columbus's *Letter* and *Journal* as well as Chanca's report included here, in order to show how the notion of *caribe*, like that of *aruaca*, continued to change and evolve in meaning, as well as to become the context for identity formation or ethnogenesis.

and Navarrete presented here. Columbus and Chanca firmly inscribe the category of *caribe* and the connection to supposed cannibalism, which, the text of Figueroa shows us, was deployed with deadly effect in the subsequent colonization of the Caribbean. The text of Pané, like that of Navarrete, is oriented to what were perceived as potentially more tractable elements of the native population. In later writings *aruacas* and *caribes* were "discovered" and described throughout northern South America, but the primal anthropology of Fray Ramón Pané's *Antiquities* and the other writings presented here were the foundation for the baleful work of conquest and colonialism that underpinned the relentless invention of our new, modern world.

Documents 1a and 1b

The Letter, and Extracts from the Journal of
Columbus's First Voyage to America (1492)

The Letter (Document 1a)

Sir:

Since I know that you will be pleased at the great success with which
Our Lord has crowned my voyage, I write this to you, from which
you will learn how in thirty-three days I reached the Indies, with
the fleet which the most illustrious King and Queen, our Sovereigns,
gave to me. There I found very many islands filled with people without number, and I have taken possession of them all for Their Highnesses by proclamation and with the royal standard unfurled, and no
objection was offered to me.

The first island I found I named San Salvador, in memory of the
Divine Majesty who has marvelously bestowed all this; the Indians
call it Guanahani. To the second I gave the name de Santa Maria
de Concepción, to the third, Ferrandina, to the fourth, Isabela, to the
fifth, Juana, and so each received a new name.[1]

The translation of Columbus's *Letter* is a revised version of an earlier translation
published in *Wild Majesty: Encounters with Caribs from Columbus to the Present Day: An Anthology,* ed. Peter Hulme and Neil L. Whitehead (Oxford: Oxford
University Press, 1992), and obviously is informed by the work of earlier translators
as well. The editor's translation of the *Letter* is based on the Spanish text published
in Gil and Varela (1984). The translation of excerpts from Columbus's *Journal* is
also a revised version of the translation published in *Wild Majesty,* and is based on
the Spanish text published in *The Diario of Christopher Columbus's First Voyage to
America,* ed. O. C. Dunn and James E. Kelley (Norman: University of Oklahoma Press,
1989).

    1. Santa Maria de Concepción is now Montserrat, Ferrandina is Long Island in
the Bahamas, Isabela is a bay on the north shore of the Dominican Republic, and Juana
is Cuba.

When I reached Juana, I followed its coast to the westward, and
I found it to be so big that I thought it must be the mainland, the
province of Cathay. And since there were neither towns nor villages
on the seashore, but small settlements only, [and] I could not speak
with the people because they all fled immediately, I went forward
on the same course, thinking that I could not fail to find great cities
or towns: and at the end of many leagues,[2] seeing that there was no
change and that the coast was bearing me northwards, which was not
what I wanted, since winter was already in the air, and I proposed to
make to the south, and moreover, the wind was carrying me forward,
I determined not to wait for a change in the weather and turned back
as far as a notable harbor, from where I sent two men inland to learn
if there were a king or great cities. They traveled three days' jour-
ney and found an infinite number of small settlements and people
without number, but nothing with organization, for which reason
they returned. I understood sufficiently from other Indians, whom
I had already captured, that this land was nothing but an island, and
I therefore followed its coast eastward for 107 leagues to the point
where it ended: from which point I saw another island to the east,
distant about eighteen leagues from the first, to the east, and to it
I at once gave the name La Spanola [Hispaniola]: and I went there
and followed its northern part, as I had followed that of Juana, to the
eastward for 188 great leagues in a straight line. This island and all
the others are very fertile to an excessive degree, and this island is
extremely so; in it there are many harbors on the coast of the sea,
beyond comparison with others that I know in Christendom, and
many rivers, good and large, which is marvelous; its lands are high;
there are in it many sierras and very high mountains, beyond comparison with the island of Tenerife, all very beautiful, of a thousand
shapes, and all accessible and filled with trees of a thousand kinds
and tall, seeming to touch the sky: and I am told that they never lose
their foliage, which I can believe, for I saw them as green and lovely
as they are in Spain in May, and some of them were flowering, some
bearing fruit, and some at another stage according to their quality.
The nightingale was singing, and other little birds of a thousand
kinds there in the month of November. There are six or eight kinds of

2. A league was taken as roughly the distance a person, or a horse, can walk in
one hour, about 3.5 miles.

palm, which are a wonder to behold because of their beautiful variety, but so are the other trees and fruits and plants. In it are marvelous pine groves, and there are very wide pastures, and there is honey, and birds of many kinds and fruits of great variety. In the interior, there are mines of metals, and the population is without number.

La Spanola is a marvel. The sierras and the mountains and the plains and the pastures and the lands perfect and so rich for plant-ing and sowing, for breeding cattle of every kind, for building towns and villages. The sea harbors here have to be seen to be believed, and there are also many great rivers, with good water, most of which bear gold. In the trees and fruits and plants, there are many differences from those on Juana: on this island, there are many spices and larger mines of gold and of other metals. The people of this island and of all the other islands which I have found and of which I have (or do not have) information all go naked, men and women, just as their mothers bore them, although some of the women cover a single place with the leaf of a plant or with a net of cotton which they make for the purpose. They have no iron or steel or weapons, nor are they fit to use them; not because they are not well built and of handsome stature, but because they are exceptionally fearful. They have no other weapons except weapons made of matured canes on the ends of which they fix a small sharp stick, and they do not dare to make use of them, many times it has happened that I have sent ashore two or three men to some town to speak with them, and although countless people have come out to see them, and as soon as they have seen my men coming closer, they have run off, a father not even waiting for his son. This is not because any harm has been done to any of them: on the contrary, at every place where I have been and have been able to talk with them, I have given them everything that I had, such as cloth and many other things, receiving nothing in exchange: but this is how they are, incurably timid. It is true that, after they become reassured and lose this fear, they are so guileless and so generous with all that they possess that no one would believe unless they had seen it. Of any possession, if they are asked for it, they never say no, on the contrary they invite the person to share it and show so much love, it is as if they would give their hearts and, whether it be of valuable or cheap, they are immediately satisfied by any trifle of whatever kind that they may be given. I prohibited giving things that were completely worthless, such as pieces of broken crockery and pieces of broken glass and ends of straps: although when they were able to get them, it seemed to them that they possessed the best jewel in the world; so it was found out that for a strap a sailor received gold to the weight of 2 1/2 castellanos, and others received much more for other things which were worth less. As for new blancas, for them they would give everything they had, although it might be two or three castellanos' weight of gold, or an arroba or two of spun cotton.[3] They even took the pieces of the broken hoops of the wine barrels and gave what they had, like animals, which seemed wrong to me and I forbade it. I gave them a thousand pleasing fine things which I had brought, in order that they might love us. And, more than that, they would become Christians and be inclined to the love and service of Their Highnesses and of the whole Castilian nation, and strive to collect and give us of the things which they have in abundance and which are necessary to us. And they do not know any sect or idolatry, except that they all believe that power and good are in the sky, and believed very firmly that I, with these ships and men, came from the sky, and in this belief they everywhere received me after they had lost their fear. This belief does not result from their being ignorant, since they are of a very acute intelligence, men who navigate all those seas, so that it is marvelous how good an account they give of everything; but rather because they have never seen people clothed or ships of such a kind. As soon as I arrived in the Indies, in the first island which I found I took some of them by force, in order that they might learn and might give me information of whatever there was in those parts, and so it was that they soon understood us, and we them, either by speech or signs: and they have been very useful. At present, those I bring with me are still of the opinion that I come from the sky, despite all the conversation which they have had with me. And these were the first to announce this wherever I went, and the others went running from house to house, and to the neighboring towns, with loud cries of "Come! Come! See the people from the sky!" So all came, men and women alike, as soon as they were confident about us; not one, small or great, remained behind, and they all brought something to eat and drink, which they gave with extraordinary affection.

3. A castellano is a gold coin, a blanca is a copper coin, and an arroba is a unit of weight equivalent to twenty-five pounds.

In all the islands, they have very many canoes, which are like rowing *fustas*,[4] some larger and some smaller, and some are greater than a *fusta*, with eighteen benches. They are not so broad, because they are made of a single log of wood, but a *fusta* would not keep up with them in rowing, since their speed is incredible; and in these they navigate all those islands, which are innumerable, and carry their merchandise. I have seen some of these canoes with seventy or eighty men in them, each one with his paddle.

In all these islands, I saw no great diversity in the appearance of the people or in their manners or language: on the contrary, they all understand one another, which is a very curious thing, on account of which I hope that Their Highnesses will determine upon their conversion to our holy faith, towards which they are much inclined. I have already said how I went 107 leagues in a straight line from west to east along the seacoast of the island Juana. On account of that voyage I can say that this island is larger than England and Scotland together, for, beyond these 107 leagues, there remain to the westward two provinces to which I have not gone, one of which they call Avon, where people are born with tails.[5] These provinces cannot have a length of less than 50 or 60 leagues, as could be understood from those Indians whom I have, and who know all the islands. The other, Hispaniola, has a circumference greater than all Spain from Colunia [Collioure] by the seacoast to Fuenteravia [Fuenterrabía] in Vizcaya [Biscay], for I went along one side for 188 great leagues in a straight line from west to east. This is a land to be desired and, once seen, never to be left. In it, although I have taken possession of all of them [the islands] for Their Highnesses, and all are more richly endowed than I know how or am able to say, and I hold all for Their Highnesses, so that they may dispose of them as they do of the kingdoms of Castile and as absolutely; [so] in this Hispaniola, in the situation most convenient and in the best district for the mines of gold and for all trade as well with the mainland here as well as with that there belonging to the Great Khan, where will be great trade and profit,

---

4. A *fusta* was a small, fast, shallow-draft vessel that used both oars and a sail. Usually it had six to nine oars with two rowers on each oar and a single mast with a triangular sail, and would be armed with several small cannon. As the *fusta* was the favorite ship of the North African corsairs of the Barbary Coast, the analogy would have been very suggestive to Columbus's contemporaries.

5. The location of this province is unknown.

I have taken possession of a large town, to which I gave the name
Villa de Navidad, and in it I have made defenses and a fort, which will
now by this time be entirely completed, and in it I have left enough
men for such a purpose with arms and artillery and provisions for
more than a year, and a *fusta*, and a master of all sea craft to build
others, and great friendship with the king of that land, so much so
that he was proud to call me brother and to treat me as such. And
even were he to change his attitude and offer offense to these people,
he and his men do not know what weapons are, and they go naked, as
I have already said. They are the most timorous people that there are
in the world, so that the men who remain there alone would suffice
to destroy all that land, and the island is without danger for their
persons, if they know how to govern themselves.

In all these islands it seems to me that all men are content with
one woman, and to their chief or king they give as many as twenty.
It appears to me that the women work more than the men. I have not
been able to find out if they hold private property; it seemed true to
me that everyone took a share in whatever anyone had, especially
with food. In these islands I have so far found no human monstrosi-
ties, as many expected, but on the contrary all the people are of fine
appearance, nor are they Negroes as in Guinea, but with flowing hair,
and they are not born where there is too much force in the rays of
the sun; it is true that the sun there has great power, although it is
distant from the equinoctial line twenty-six degrees. In these islands,
where there are high mountains, the cold was severe this winter, but
they endure it, being used to it and with the help of meats [which]
they eat with many and excessively hot spices. Thus I have found no
monsters, nor report of any, except of an island which is Carib, which
is the second at the entrance into the Indies, which is inhabited by
a people who are regarded in all the islands as very ferocious, [and]
who eat human flesh. They have many canoes, with which they range
through all the islands of India, [and] rob and take whatever they can.
They are no more malformed than the others, except that they have
the custom of wearing their hair long like women, and they use bows
and arrows of the same cane stems, with a small piece of wood at the
end, owing to their lack of iron, which they do not possess. They are
ferocious among these other people, who are cowardly to an excessive
degree, but I make no more account of them than of the rest. These

are they who have intercourse with the women of Matinino,[6] which is the first island found after leaving Spain for the Indies, in which there is not a man. These women engage in no feminine occupation, but use bows and arrows of cane, like those already mentioned, and they arm and protect themselves with plates of copper, of which they have much. In another island, which they assure me is larger than Hispaniola, the people have no hair. In it there is incalculable gold, and from it and from the other islands I bring with me Indians as evidence.

In conclusion, to speak only of what has been accomplished on this voyage, which was so hasty, Their Highnesses can see that I will give them as much gold as they may need, if Their Highnesses will render me very slight assistance; presently, I will give them spices and cotton, as much as Their Highnesses shall command; and mastic, as much as they shall order shipped and which, up to now, has been found only in Greece, in the island of Chios, and the Seigniory [the government of Naples] sells it for what it pleases; and aloe, as much as they shall order to be shipped; and slaves, as many as they shall order, and who will be from among the idolaters. I believe also that I have found rhubarb and cinnamon, and I shall find a thousand other things of value, which the people whom I have left there will have found, for I have not delayed anywhere, provided the wind allowed me to sail, except in Villa de Navidad, so as to leave it secured and well established. And in truth I would have done much more if the ships had served me as justice demanded. This is sufficient, and [illegible] the eternal God, Our Lord, who gives to all those who walk in His way victory over things which appear impossible. And this was notably one, for, although these lands have been talked or written of, all was conjectural, without [our] getting sight of them, but amounted only to this, that those who heard for the most part listened and judged rather by hearsay than from anything else. So that, since Our Redeemer gave this victory to our most illustrious King and Queen, and to their renowned kingdoms, in so great a matter, for this all Christendom ought to feel delight and make great feasts and give solemn thanks to the Holy Trinity, with many solemn

---

6. Matinino may be mythical, or may be the island of Martinique. See the discussion of the Amazon myth cycle in the introduction.

prayers for the great exaltation which they shall have in the turning of so many peoples to our holy faith, and afterwards for the temporal benefits, because not only Spain but all Christendom will here have refreshment and gain.

This is what has been done, though in brief.

Done in the caravel, off the Canary Islands, On the fifteenth day of February, in the year 1493.

At your orders.

The Admiral

After having written this, and being in the sea of Castile, there came upon me so great a south and southeast wind that I was obliged to ease the ships, but I ran here today into this port of Lisbon, which was the greatest marvel in the world, whence I decided to write to Their Highnesses. In all the Indies I have always found weather as in May. There I went in thirty-three days and I returned in twenty-eight, except that these storms have detained me for fourteen days, boating about in this sea. Here all the sailors say that never has there been so bad a winter nor so many ships lost.

Done on the fourteenth day of March.

The Journal (Document 1b)

Friday 23 November

All today the Admiral steered towards the land to the south, always with some wind, but the current stopped him from reaching it; instead he was as far from it at sunset as in the morning. The wind was east-northeast and right for going south, but it was slight, and beyond this cape appeared another land or cape which also runs to the east, which the Indians he was carrying with him called Bohio [Hispaniola]; they said it was very large and that on it there were people who had one eye in their foreheads,[7] and others that were called *canibales*, of whom they showed great fear. He says that when

7. The ancestral serpent spirit of the Caribs of Dominica had a monstrous, optical jewel protruding from its head; see also reference in the account of Ramón Pané.

they saw that he was taking this course, they could not speak because they feared these people would eat them, and are well armed. The Admiral says that he truly believes there was something in this, although since they were armed they must be people with reason; and he believed that they must have captured some of them, and because those people did not return to their lands they would say that they [the *canibales*] ate them. They believed the same thing about the Christians and about the Admiral the first time some of them saw them. . . .

Monday 26 November

At sunrise he raised anchor from the harbor at Santa Cathalina, where he was behind the flat island, and sailed along the coast with a slight southwesterly wind in the direction of the Cabo del Pico, which was to the southeast. He arrived late at the cape because the wind dropped, and having arrived he saw to the southeast by east another cape which was about sixty miles away; and from there he saw another cape that lay toward the southeast by south from the ship, which seemed to him about twenty miles away, to which he gave the name of Cabo de Campana, which he could not reach during the day because the wind completely died down again. In that whole day he sailed about thirty-two miles, which is eight leagues, within which distance he noted and marked nine distinct harbors, which all the crew thought wonderful, and five large rivers, since he always sailed close to the land in order to see everything well. All of that land is made up of very high and beautiful mountains, not dry nor rocky, but all accessible and with very beautiful valleys. The valleys, like the mountains, were full of tall and leafy trees, delightful to look at; and it seemed that many of them were pine groves. And also, behind the said Cabo del Pico to the southeast, there are two islets, each of which is two leagues around, and behind them three wonderful harbors and two big rivers. Along all of this coast he saw no settlements from the sea: it may be that there were some, and there were signs of this because, wherever they went ashore, they found signs of people and many fires. He judged that the land that he saw today on the southeast part of the Cabo de Campana was the island that the Indians called Bohio, and it seemed to be so because the said

cape is separated from that land.[8] All the people that he has found up
to today, he says, are very frightened of those *caniba*, or *canima*, and
they say that they live on this island of Bohio, which must be very
large, it seems to him; and he believes that they [the *caniba*] will take
them to their lands and villages since they are very cowardly and
know nothing about weapons. And because of this it seems to him
that those Indians he was bringing with him do not usually settle on
the coast because of being close to this land. He says that after they
saw him take the route to this land they could not speak, fearing that
they would have them to eat; and he could not still their fear. And
they say that they [the *canibales*] only have one eye and the face of
a dog; and the Admiral thought they were lying and felt that those
who captured them must have been under the dominion of the Great
Khan. . . .

Wednesday 5 December

All this night he beat about off Cabo Lindo,[9] where he spent the
night in order to see the land, which ran to the east, and at sunrise
he saw another cape two leagues to the east. Beyond that one, he saw
that the coast turned to the south and tended southwest, and he soon
saw a very beautiful and tall cape in the same direction, seven leagues
from the other one. He would have liked to go there, but because of
his desire to go to the island of Baneque [Jamaica?], which lay to the
northeast according to what the Indians he had with him said, he did
not; and he could not go to Baneque either, because the wind he had
was northeast. Proceeding in this way, he looked to the southeast
and saw land, and it was a very big island, of which he says he had
already received information from the Indians, and which they call
Bohio, inhabited by people of whom, he says, those of Cuba, or Juana,
and of all the other islands have great fear because, he says, they eat
men. These Indians told him other very marvelous things by signs;
but the Admiral does not say that he believes them, only that the
people of that island of Bohio must be shrewder and more intelligent
than they to capture them, because these are very faint of heart. So,

8. Santa Cathalina is Isla Catalina, off the southeastern coast of what is now the
Dominican Republic. The other places in this paragraph cannot be determined with
certainty, but seem to refer to Hispianola.

9. Evidently also in Hispianola.

because the weather was from the northeast and shifting north, he decided to leave Cuba, or Juana, which until now he had taken for Tierra Firme[10] because of its size, since he had gone fully 120 leagues along one side. And he departed to the southeast by east since the land he had seen tended southeast. He took this precaution because the wind always went around from the north to the northeast and from there to the east and southeast. The wind blew hard and he put on all sails, the sea being smooth and the current helping him, so that from morning until an hour after midday he made eight miles an hour, and this was for six hours, although not quite, because he says that there the nights were nearly fifteen hours long.[11]

Afterwards he went at ten miles an hour, and thus up to sunset he made eighty-eight miles, which are twenty-two leagues, all to the southeast; and because night was approaching he ordered the caravel *Nina* to go ahead to look at the harbor in daylight, because she was fast. And when she reached the mouth of the harbor, which was like the Bay of Cadiz, and because it was night, she sent her boat, which carried a lantern, to sound the harbor; and before the Admiral reached where the caravel was tacking back and forth and waiting for the boat to make signals that it should enter the harbor, the light on the boat went out. The caravel, when it saw no light, ran out to sea and showed a light to the Admiral, and when they came up to her, told him what had happened. At this point those on the boat lit another light. The caravel went to it and the Admiral could not, and passed all that night beating about. . . .

Tuesday 11 December

He did not leave because of the wind, which was still east and northeast. Facing that harbor, as has been said, is the island of Tortuga, and it appears to be a large island; and the coast of it runs almost like that of Hispaniola, and there can be from one to the other at most ten leagues; that is to say, from the cape of Cinquin to the head of Tortuga, which is to the north of Hispaniola.[12] Farther along, its coast runs south. He says that he wanted to see that passage between

10. A general term to denote a major landmass, this became the name for the South American continent.
11. In fact the average length of day is about eleven hours in these latitudes.
12. The location of the cape of Cinquin is unknown.

these two islands in order to see the island of Hispaniola, which is the most beautiful thing in the world; and because, as the Indians that he brought told him, this was the way one had to go to the island of Baneque. They told him that it was a very large island with big mountains and rivers and valleys, and they said that the island of Bohio was larger than Juana, which they call Cuba, and that it is not surrounded by water. And they seem to mean that it is the mainland that is here beyond Hispaniola, which they call *caritaba*, and which is a thing of infinite size. And perhaps they are right, for they may be preyed on by cunning people, because all these islands live in great fear of those from Caniba.[13] And so I say again what I have said on other occasions, he says, that *Caniba* is nothing else but the people of the Great Khan, who must be very near here. And they have ships and come to capture them, and since they do not return they believe that they have been eaten. Each day we understand these Indians better and they us, since many times they have confused one thing for another, says the Admiral. He sent men ashore, where they found much mastic, uncongealed. He says that the rains must cause this, and that in Chios they gather it around March and that in these lands they would collect it in January, since they are so temperate. They caught many fish like those of Castile: dace, salmon, hake, dory, pompano, mullet, corbina, shrimp;[14] and they saw sardines. They found much aloe. . . .

Monday 17 December

That night the wind blew strongly from the east-northeast. The sea did not get very rough because the island of Tortuga, which is opposite and forms a shelter, protected and guarded it. So he remained there that day. He sent the sailors to fish with nets; the Indians relaxed with the Christians and brought them arrows of the kind

13.   The term *caniba* is said by Columbus to refer to both a possible place and to people he thought his native informants were describing. Adding to this lack of precision is Columbus's allusion to the term *caritaba*. It is also evident from this passage that Columbus is trying to reconcile expectations about finding an oriental "Khan" with the speech acts of those he encounters in the Caribbean.

14.   The pompano is one of various kinds of fish found in the tropical and temperate Atlantic.

from *caniba* or of the *canibales;* and they are made from spikes of cane, and they insert into them little sticks, fired and sharp, and they are very long. Two men showed them [the Christians] that pieces of flesh were missing from their bodies, and gave them to understand that the *canibales* had taken mouthfuls from them. The Admiral did not believe it. He again sent some Christians to the town, and in exchange for small glass beads they secured some pieces of gold worked into thin leaf. They saw one man whom the Admiral took for governor of that land or a province of it, called *cacique,* with a piece as large as a hand of that sheet of gold, and it seems that he wanted to trade it. He went off to his house and the others remained in the square; and he had small pieces of that sheet made and, bringing one piece at a time, traded for it.

When none was left, he said by signs that he had sent for more and that the next day they would bring it. All these things, and the manner of them, and their customs and mildness and behavior show them to be people more alert and intelligent than others they had found up to that time, the Admiral says. In the afternoon a canoe came here from the island of Tortuga with fully forty men, and when it reached the beach all the people of the town who were there sat down together as a sign of peace, and some of those from the canoe, almost all of them, came ashore. The *cacique* alone got up and, with words that seemed threatening, made them return to the canoe, and threw water on them and took stones from the beach and threw them in the water, and after all of them very obediently got into the canoe and set off, he took a stone and put it in the hand of my bailiff for him to throw it. I had sent him and the clerk and others ashore to see if they would bring back anything advantageous. The bailiff did not want to throw the stone at them. There the *cacique* showed how much he favored the Admiral. The canoe soon went away, and, after it had gone, they told the Admiral that on Tortuga there was more gold than on Hispaniola because it was closer to Baneque. The Admiral said that he did not believe that there were gold mines on Hispaniola or Tortuga, but that they brought it from Baneque, and that they brought little because the people had nothing to give for it. And that land is so rich that there is no need to work hard to get sustenance or clothing, since they go around naked. And the Admiral believed that he was very near the source and that Our Lord would show him where the gold comes from. He had information that from there to Baneque would take four days, which would be thirty or forty leagues, so that they could get there in one day of good weather. . . .

[After the shipwreck of the Santa Maria, Columbus *is visited by the local* cacique *on the north coast of what is now Haiti.]*

Wednesday 26 December

Today at sunrise the king of that land, who was in that place, came to the caravel *Nina,* where the Admiral was, and almost weeping said to him that he should not grieve, for he would give him all that he had, and that he had given the Christians who were on land two very large houses, and that he would give them more if they were needed, and as many canoes as could load and unload the ship and put on land as many people as he wanted, and that he had done so yesterday without a crumb of bread or any other thing at all being taken; so faithful are they (says the Admiral), and without greed for what is another's, and so, more than them all, was that virtuous king. While the Admiral was talking to him, another canoe came from another place bringing certain pieces of gold which they wanted to give for a bell, because they desired nothing so much as bells, for the canoe was not yet alongside when they called and showed the pieces of gold, saying *chuq chuque* for bells, for they almost go mad for them. After having seen this, and the canoes from the other places leaving, they called to the Admiral and asked him to order one bell kept until the next day, because they would bring four pieces of gold as large as a hand. The Admiral rejoiced to hear this, and afterwards a sailor who came from ashore told the Admiral it was marvelous to see the pieces of gold that the Christians who were on land haggled for a trifle. For a lace end [aiguelette] they gave pieces that would be more than two castellanos, and that was now nothing compared to what it would be after a month. The king rejoiced greatly to see the Admiral happy, and understood that he wanted a lot of gold; and he told him by signs that he knew where there was very much, near there, in great quantities; and he should be of good heart, that he would give him as much gold as he wanted. And, about this, the Admiral says that he gave him a report and, in particular, that there was gold in Cipango, which they call Cybao, in such quantity that they hold it as of no account and that he would bring it there, although also that in that island of Hispaniola, which they call Bohio, and in that province Caribata there was much more of it.[15] The king ate on the caravel with the Admiral, and afterwards went ashore with him, where he did the Admiral much honor and gave him refreshments of two or three kinds of green pepper with shrimp and game and other foods which they had and some of their bread, which they called *cacabi*.[16] From there he took him to see some groves of trees near the houses, and a good thousand people, all naked, walked there with him. The lord was now wearing the shirt and gloves that the Admiral had given him; and he was more delighted with the gloves than with anything else that he was given. In his way of eating, his honest manners, and attractive cleanliness, he showed himself certainly to be of some lineage. After having eaten, for he spent a long time at table, they brought certain herbs with which they rubbed their hands a great deal (the Admiral thought they did it to soften them), and they gave him water for his hands. After they finished, he took the Admiral to the beach, and the Admiral sent for a Turkish bow and a handful of arrows: and he had one of the men of his company who knew how to, shoot it; and to the lord, since he did not know what weapons are, because they do not have and do not use them, it appeared a great thing, although he says that at the beginning there was talk about those of Caniba, whom they call *caribes*, who come to take them and who carry bows and arrows without iron, for in all of those lands they have no knowledge of it or of steel or of any other metal except gold and copper, although of copper the Admiral had seen but little. The Admiral told him by signs that the sovereigns of Castile would order the *caribes* destroyed, and they would order all of them to be brought with hands bound. The Admiral ordered a lombard and a spingard[17] to be fired, and seeing the effect that their force had, and how they penetrated, he was astonished. And when his people heard the shots they all fell to the ground. They brought the Admiral a large mask that had large pieces of gold in the ears and eyes and on other parts, which the king gave him with other gold jewels that he

15. Cipango is a name for Japan; the place Columbus refers to may be mythical. Caribata is the continental mainland (Tierra Firme).

16. *Cacabi* is cassava (*Manihot esculenta*), the staple root crop of tropical America.

17. The lombard was a large cannon; the spingard (*espingarda*), much smaller, was the forerunner of the blunderbuss.

himself put on the Admiral's head and around his neck: and to the other Christians who were with him he also gave many things. The Admiral was greatly pleased and consoled by these things that he saw; and the anguish and sorrow that he had suffered and felt because of the loss of the ship were assuaged and he recognized that Our Lord had caused the ship to run aground there so that he would found a settlement there. And to this end (he says) so many things came to hand that truly it was no disaster, but great fortune, because it is certain, he says, that if I had not gone aground I would have passed by without anchoring at this place, because it is situated here within a wide bay, and in it two or three sandbars: nor on this voyage would I have left people here: nor, even had I wished to leave them, could I have given them so many supplies or so many tools or so many provisions or materials for a fortress. And it is very true that many of the people who are here have begged me and have had others beg me to be willing to give them permission to stay. Now I have ordered built a tower and a fort, all of the best, and a big moat, not that I believe this necessary for these people, for it is obvious that with these men I have with me I would subdue all this island, which I believe is larger than Portugal and double or more in people: they are naked and without arms and very cowardly beyond remedy. But it is right that this tower be built and that it be as it should be, being so far from Their Highnesses, so that they get to know the skills of Their Highnesses' people and what they can do, so that they will obey them with love and fear. And so they have boards with which to build all the fortress, and provisions of bread and wine for more than a year, and seeds to sow, and the ship's boat, and a caulker and a carpenter and a gunner and a cooper: and many men among them who greatly desire to serve Their Highnesses and to please me by finding out about the mine where gold is collected. So everything has worked out just right for this beginning to be made, and above all, when the ship ran aground, it was so softly that it was almost not felt, nor was there wave nor wind. All this the Admiral says. And he adds more to show that it was great good fortune and the particular will of God that the ship should run aground there so that he would leave people there; and he says that if it had not been for the treachery of the master and of the men, all or most of whom were from the same place as he, not wanting to cast the anchor astern in order to get the ship off, as the Admiral ordered them, the ship would have been saved and so he would not have been able to find out about the country (he says) as he did in those days that he was there, and in future through those whom he resolved to leave, because he always went with the intention to explore and not to stop anywhere more than a day, save for lack of wind, because the ship (he says) was very slow and not suited for exploration; and in taking such a ship (he says) the men of Palos failed to fulfill their promise to the King and Queen to provide suitable ships for that voyage, and they did not do it. The Admiral ends by saying that of everything that was in the ship not even a lace end was lost, neither plank nor nail, because she remained as sound as when she set out, except that she was cut and somewhat opened up to get out the water butts and all the merchandise, all of which they put on land and guarded well, as has been said. And he says that he trusts in God that on the return that he intended to make from Castile he would find a barrel of gold which those whom he had left would have obtained by barter, and that they would have found the gold mine and the spices, and those things in such quantity that the sovereigns, within three years, would undertake and prepare to go and conquer the Holy Sepulcher; for thus (he says) I urged Their Highnesses that all the profits of this my enterprise should be spent on the conquest of Jerusalem, and Their Highnesses laughed and said that it would please them and that even without this they had that desire. These are the words of the Admiral. . . .

Saturday 12 January

At the dawn watch he steered east with a fresh wind and proceeded like this until daylight, and during this time made twenty miles and in the following two hours made twenty-four miles. From there he saw land to the south and went toward it; he was about forty-eight miles from it. He says that, keeping the ship a safe distance from shore, at night he made twenty-eight miles to the north-northeast. When he saw land, he named a cape that he sighted Cabo de Padre y Hijo [Cape Father and Son] because at its eastern point it has two headlands, one larger than the other. Later, two leagues to the east, he saw a large and very beautiful opening between two big mountains, and he saw that it was a very large and good harbor with an excellent entrance. But because it was very early in the morning, and so as not to lose distance, because most of the time in that part east winds

blow, and at that time he had a north-northwesterly, he did not want
to stop but continued his course to the east as far as a very high and
very beautiful cape all of sheer rock, to which he gave the name Cabo
del Enamorado, which was thirty-two miles to the east of that harbor
which he called Puerto Sacro.[18] And when he reached it he discovered
another cape much more beautiful and higher and rounded, all of
rock, just like the Cabo de San Vicente in Portugal; and it was twelve
miles to the east of the Enamorado. After getting to a position level
with the Enamorado, he saw, between it and the other cape, that a
large bay was formed, which had a width of three leagues and in the
middle of it a tiny little islet. The depth is great at the entrance right
the way up to the shore. He anchored there in twelve fathoms; he
sent the boat ashore for water and to see if they could communicate;
but the people all fled. He also anchored to see if all that land was
continuous with Hispaniola or whether, as he suspected, what he had
called a gulf might not form another island by itself. He remained
amazed that the island of Hispaniola was so big.

Sunday 13 January

He did not leave this harbor, because there was no land breeze with
which to leave; he would have liked to leave to go to another better
harbor because that one was somewhat open, and because he wanted
to observe how the conjunction of the moon with the sun that he
expected on the seventeenth of this month would turn out, and its
opposition with Jupiter and conjunction with Mercury, and the sun
in opposition to Jupiter, which is the cause of great winds. He sent
the boat ashore at a beautiful beach so they could take some green
peppers to eat, and they found some men with bows and arrows with
whom they stopped to talk, and they bought from them two bows
and many arrows and asked one of them to go to speak with the
Admiral in the caravel, and he came. The Admiral says that he was
very ill proportioned in appearance, more so than others that he had
seen. He had his face all stained with charcoal, although everywhere
they are accustomed to staining themselves with different colors.
He wore all his hair very long, drawn back and tied behind, and then
gathered in a small net of parrot feathers; and he was as naked as

18. Evidently in Hispaniola.

the others. The Admiral judged that he must be of the *caribes* who eat men, and that the gulf that he had seen yesterday separated the land, and that it must be an island by itself. He asked him about the *caribes*, and he [the Indian] pointed to the east near there, which land the Admiral says that he saw yesterday before entering that bay; and the Indian told him that over there was a great deal of gold, pointing to the poop of the caravel, which was quite large, [meaning] that there were pieces that big. He called gold *tuob* and did not understand *caona*, as they call it in the first part of the island, nor *noçay* as they called it in San Salvador and in the other islands. In Hispaniola they call filigree, a base gold, *tuob*. Of the island of Matinino that Indian said that it was entirely peopled by women, without men, and that in it there is very much *tuob*, which is gold, or filigree, and that it is farther to the east of Carib. He also spoke of the island of Goanin,[19] where there is much *tuob*. The Admiral says that some days ago he received news of these islands from many people. The Admiral also says that on the islands he passed they were greatly fearful of Carib and on some they called it Caniba, but on Hispaniola, Carib; and they [the *caribes*] must be a daring people since they travel through all these islands and eat the people they can take. He says that he understood some words, and through them he says he found out other things, and that the Indians he brought with him understood more, although they found differences between the languages, because of the great distance between the lands. He had the Indian given something to eat, and he gave him pieces of green and red cloth and glass beads, of which they are very fond, and sent him back ashore and told him to bring gold if he had it, which he believed he did, because of some little things that he was wearing. When the boat reached shore, behind the trees there were a good fifty-five naked men with very long hair, just like the women wear it in Castile. On the backs of their heads they wore plumes of parrot feathers and of other birds, and each one was carrying his bow. The Indian landed and made the others leave their bows and arrows and a piece of wood that is like a very heavy [illegible] that they carry in place of a sword.[20] Later they came to the boat and the men in the boat went ashore and began to buy from them the bows and arrows and other arms, because the Admiral

19.   Probably a reference to the mainland region known as Guayana in native languages, an important source of native metallurgy.

20.   That is, a war club, *aputu* or *mossi*.

had so ordered. When two bows were sold, they did not want to give any more: instead, they prepared to attack the Christians and capture them. They went running to pick up their bows and arrows where they had laid them aside and came back with ropes in their hands, in order, he says, to tie up the Christians. Seeing them come running toward them, the Christians, being prepared (because the Admiral was always warning them about this), attacked them, and they gave one Indian a great slash across the buttocks and another they wounded in the chest with a crossbow shot. Having seen by this that they could achieve little, even though the Christians were seven and they fifty odd, they fled leaving arrows here and another his bows there, so that none remained. He says that the Christians would have killed many of them if the pilot who went as their captain had not prevented it. The Christians then returned to the caravel with their boat: and when the Admiral found out, he said that on the one hand he was pleased and on the other not. [He was pleased] because they would fear the Christians, since without doubt (he says) the people there are evildoers and he believed they were those of Carib, and that they would eat men. Because if the boat that he had left for the thirty-nine men in the fortress and town of Navidad came there, they would be frightened of doing them any harm. And if they are not of those *caribes*, at least they must be their neighbors and with the same customs and be men without fear, not like the others of the other islands, who are cowards and, beyond understanding, without weapons. All of this the Admiral says, and that he would like to take some of them. He says they made many smoke signals, as was the custom in that island of Hispaniola.

Monday 14 January

He would have liked to send out a party this night in search of the houses of those Indians to capture some of them, believing that they were *caribes*, but for the strong east and northeast wind and the high sea it caused [he could not do so]. But when day came they saw many Indians on the shore, because of which the Admiral ordered the boat to go there with well-equipped men. The Indians quickly came up to the stern of the boat, and especially the Indian who, the day before, had come to the caravel and to whom the Admiral had given the trinkets for barter. With him, he says, came a king who had given some beads to the said Indian to give to the men in the boat as a sign of security and peace. This king, with three of his men, entered the boat and came to the caravel. The Admiral ordered them to be given biscuit and honey to eat, and he gave him [the king] a red cap and beads and a piece of red cloth: and to the others also pieces of cloth. The king said that tomorrow he would bring a gold mask, affirming that there was much gold there and in Carib, and in Matinino. Afterwards he sent them ashore well contented. The Admiral also says that the caravels were leaking heavily around the keel and complained greatly about the caulkers, who had caulked them very badly in Palos: and that when they saw that the Admiral realized the deficiency of their work and wanted to make them put it right, they fled. But despite the large amount of water the caravels were taking on, he trusted in Our Lord who brought him [here] to return him because of His pity and mercy, for His High Majesty well knew how much controversy he had at first before he was able to set out from Castile, and that no one else was in his favor except Him, because He knew his heart, and after God, Their Highnesses.[21] And all the others had been against him without any reason at all. And he says more as follows: and they have been the cause that the royal crown of Your Highnesses does not have a revenue of a hundred millions more than it has, since I came to serve you, which is now seven years ago on 20 January this very month, and more that would be added from now onwards. But that powerful God will make all well. These are his words.

Tuesday 15 January

He says that he wants to leave because there is no benefit in staying, because of the difficulties with, he should say the outrage toward, the Indians. He also says that today he has found out that all the abundance of gold was in the region of Their Highnesses' town of Navidad, and that on the island of Carib, there was much filigree, and in Matinino too, although it will be difficult in Carib because those people, he says, eat human flesh, and that from there their island was visible, and he had resolved to go to it since it is on the way, and to that of Matinino, which, he says, was entirely populated by women without men, to see both and to take, he says, some of them.

---

21. The original passage is unclear here.

The Admiral sent the boat ashore, and the king of that land had not come because, he says, the town was distant, but he sent his crown of gold as he had promised, and many other men came with cotton and with bread and peppers, all with their bows and arrows. After they had bartered everything, he says that four young men came to the caravel, and they seemed to the Admiral to give such a good account of all those islands to the east on the same route that the Admiral had to follow, that he decided to take them to Castile with him. He says that they have no iron or other metal that has been seen, although in a few days not much can be learned about a country, owing to the difficulty of the language, which the Admiral did not understand except through guesswork, and because they did not know in a few days what he was trying to do. The bows of that people, he says, were as big as those in France and England; the arrows are just like the spears of other people he had seen up to that time, which are made from shoots of canes when planted,[22] which remain very straight for the length of one or two yards. And afterwards they put at the end a piece of sharp wood, a palm and a half long, and on top of this little stick some insert a fish tooth, and some, the most, put poison there. And they do not shoot as in other places, but in a certain way that cannot do much harm. There was very much cotton there, very fine and long, and there are many mastic trees, and it seemed to him that the bows were made of yew and that there is gold and copper. There is also much *chili*, which is their pepper, of a sort worth more than pepper, and nobody eats without it because they find it very healthy. Fifty caravels can be loaded with it each year in that Hispaniola. He says that he found much weed in that bay, of the kind they found in the gulf when he came on the discovery, because of which he believes that there were islands to the east, even directly from where he began to find them, because he considers it certain that that weed grows in shallow water near land; and he says that if this is so, these Indies are very near the Canary Islands, and for this reason he believed that they were less than four hundred leagues distant.

---

22. The original passage is unclear here.

Document 2

The Report of Diego Chanca on Columbus's
Second Voyage to America (1494)

. . . On the morning of the Sunday before mentioned,[1] we saw an
island ahead of the ships, and then another came into view on the
right-hand side. The first was a high and mountainous land on the
side we saw; the other was flat and also covered with dense woods;
and when it grew lighter, islands began to appear on one side and
on the other, so that during that day six islands were seen in different directions, most of them very large. We steered directly to look
at the one which we had first sighted[2] and reached the coast, going
more than a league in search of a harbor to anchor in, but we could
not find one. What we saw of the island was very beautiful, and there
were very verdant mountains, right down to the shore, which was
delightful to see, since in our own country at that season there is
scarcely any green. As we found no harbor, the Admiral decided that
we should go back to the other island, which appeared on the right
hand, four or five leagues distance from the first. Meanwhile one
ship remained off the first island, awaiting our return, looking for a
harbor all that day, and found there a good harbor and saw houses
and people. And later that night our ship came back to join the fleet,
which had put into harbor at the other island,[3] where the Admiral,
with the royal standard in his hands, landed, and many men with
him, and there took possession for Their Highnesses according to
the law. On this island the trees were so dense that it was marvelous, and there were such astounding varieties of trees, unknown to

The translation of Chanca's *Letter* is based on an earlier translation published in *Wild
Majesty: Encounters with Caribs from Columbus to the Present Day: An Anthology*, ed. Peter Hulme and Neil L. Whitehead (Oxford: Oxford University Press, 1992).
It is based on the Spanish text in Gil and Varela (1984).
1. November 3, 1493.
2. Dominica.
3. Marie Galante.

anyone, some with fruit, some with flowers, so that everything was verdant. There we found a tree whose leaf had the finest scent of cloves that I have ever encountered, and it resembled laurel, except that it was not so large; I think, however, that it was a species of laurel. There were wild fruits of different kinds [manchineel?], which some unwisely tasted, and though they only touched them with their tongues, the taste made their faces swell up and such a great heat and pain came over them that they seemed to be going mad; they cured this with cold things. In this island we found no people, and no sign of any; we believed it to be uninhabited. We were there some two hours, for when we arrived there it was late evening.

Then in the morning of the next day we left for another island, which appeared beyond this one some seven or eight leagues distant and which was very large.[4] We reached it near the side of a large mountain which seemed to want to touch the sky, in the middle of which was a peak even higher than all the rest of the mountain; from this peak many waters flowed in different directions, particularly in the direction where we were sailing. From three leagues away, there appeared a waterfall as broad as an ox, which hurled itself from such a height that it seemed to fall from the sky; it was visible from so far away that many bets were laid aboard the ships, some saying that it was white rocks and others that it was water. As we came nearer the truth was clear, and it was the loveliest thing in the world to see from what a height it fell and how from such a small crevice sprang such a great waterfall. When we came near, the Admiral ordered a light caravel to coast farther along to look for a harbor. It went ahead and, having reached land, sighted some houses. The captain went ashore in the boat and reached the houses, in which he found their inhabitants. As soon as they saw them [our men] they fled, and he entered their houses and searched their possessions, for they had left everything, and he took two very large parrots, quite different from all those seen before. He found much cotton, spun and ready for spinning, and articles of food; and he brought away a little of everything; in particular he collected four or five bones from the arms and legs of men. When we saw this, we suspected that the islands were those of Caribe, which are inhabited by people who eat human flesh.

Following the directions as to the position of those islands which the Indians of the islands previously discovered had given to the

4. Guadeloupe

Admiral on his former voyage, he had purposely directed his course to find them; because they were nearer to Spain, and also because from there lay the most direct route to Hispaniola, where he had left people before. We came to these islands, by the goodness of God and by the good judgment of the Admiral, as directly as if had had been sailing on a known and well-followed route.

This island is very large, and on this side it appeared that the coast was twenty-five leagues in length; we coasted along it for more than two leagues, looking for a harbor. In the direction toward which we were going, there were very high mountains; in the direction which we were leaving, wide plains appeared, and on the seashore there were some small settlements, and as soon as they [the inhabitants] saw the sails, they all ran away. Having gone two leagues, we found a harbor at last. That night the Admiral decided that at dawn someone should go to speak with them and to find out what people they were, despite feeling suspicious as the ones seen running away were naked people, like the ones the Admiral had already seen on the first voyage.

That morning certain captains set out; some returned at the hour of eating and brought a boy of about fourteen, as was afterwards learned, and he said that he was one of those whom these people held captive. The others divided up. Some captured a small boy, whom a man had been leading by the hand and had left behind in order to escape. They then sent him with one group; the others remained, and they captured certain women, natives of the island, and other women who were among the prisoners, who came willingly. From this party, one captain, not knowing that there had been any communication, went off with six men and got lost along with his companions, so that they never found the way back until, after four days, they reached the coast and, by following it, came back to the fleet again. We had already given them up for lost and eaten by those people who are called the *caribes*, for there was no reason to think that they were lost in any other way, since there were among them naval pilots, who know by the star[5] how to come and go from Spain; and we thought that in so small a place they could not get lost.

On this first day that we landed there, many men and women walked along the shore next to the water looking at the fleet and marveling at something so novel. And when a boat landed came to

5. The pole star.

speak with them, saying to them *taino, taino,* which means good, they waited as long as they [the crew] remained in the water, staying close, so that they could flee when they wanted to. As a result none of the men could be taken by force or persuasion, except two who felt confident and were then taken by force. More than twenty women from among the captives were taken, and other native women of the island came of their own accord and were captured and taken by force. Some boys, prisoners, came to us, escaping from the natives of the island who held them captive.

We were in this harbor eight days, because of the loss of the above-mentioned captain, and we often went on land, going about their dwellings and villages which were on the coast, finding an infinite number of men's bones and skulls hung up about the houses like vessels to hold things. Not many men appeared here, the reason being, according to what the women told us, that ten canoes had gone with people to raid other islands. These people seemed to us more polished than those who live in the other islands which we have seen, although they all have dwellings of straw, but these have them much better made and better provided with supplies, and there seems to be in them more industry, both male and female. They had much cotton, spun and ready for spinning, and many cotton cloths, so well made that they lose nothing by comparison with those of our own country.

We asked the women who were captive on this island what these people were; they replied that they were *caribes.* After they understood that we hated those people for their evil custom of eating the flesh of men, they rejoiced greatly, and if after that they brought any woman or man of the *caribes,* they said secretly that they were *caribes,* for even here where all were in our power they went in fear of them, like subjugated people; and so we found out which of the women were *caribes* and which not, for the *caribe* women wear two rings made of cotton on each leg, one near the knee and the other near the ankle, so that the calves are made large and the places mentioned very constricted, and it seems to me that they regard this as something graceful; so by this difference we know the ones from the others.

The way of life of these *caribe* people is bestial. There are three islands; this one is called Turuqueira, the other, which we saw first, is called Ceyre, and the third is called Ayai. They are all agreed, as if they were of one lineage, to do no harm to each other. They make war together on all the other neighboring islands, going 150 leagues by sea to make raids in the many canoes which they have, which are small *fustas* made of a single piece of wood. Their arms are arrows rather than iron weapons, because they do not possess any iron; they fix on points made of tortoiseshell, others from another island fix on fish bones which are jagged, being like that naturally, like very strong saws, a thing which to an unarmed people, as they all are, can kill and do great injury, but by people of our nation are not arms greatly to be feared. These people raid the other islands and carry off the women whom they can take, especially the young and beautiful ones, whom they keep to serve them and have them as concubines, and they carry off so many that in fifty houses nobody was found, and of the captives more than twenty were young girls. These women also say that they are treated with a cruelty which seems incredible, for sons whom they [the *caribes*] have from them are eaten and they rear only those whom they have from their native women. The men whom they are able to take, those who are alive they bring to their houses to butcher for meat, and those who are dead are eaten there and then. They say that men's flesh is so good that there is nothing like it in the world, and it certainly seems so, for the bones which we found in these houses had been gnawed of everything they could gnaw,[6] so that nothing was left on them except what was much too tough to be eaten. In one house there a man's neck was found cooking in a pot. They cut off the male member of the boys they take prisoner and make use of them until they are men, and then when they want to make a feast, they kill and eat them, for they say that the flesh of boys and of women is not good to eat. Of these boys, three came fleeing to us, and all three had had their members cut off.

After four days, the captain who had got lost returned. We had already despaired of his coming back, since other groups had already gone twice to look for them, and on that very day one group had just come back without having discovered any definite news of them. We rejoiced at their return as if they had been newly found. This captain, besides those who went with him, brought in ten head, boys and women. Neither they nor the others who went to look for them ever

---

6. Defleshing of bones was a standard funerary practice for the custom of secondary burial, which is found widely throughout the Americas, so not necessarily evidence of cannibalism as Chanca infers.

found men, because they had fled or perhaps it was because in that region there were few men, because, as was learned from the women, ten canoes with people had gone to raid other islands. He and those who went with him came from the mountain so broken that it was sad to see them. When they were asked how they had got lost, they said that the trees were so thick that they could not see the sky, and that some of them, who were sailors, had climbed the trees to look for the [pole] star and had never been able to see it, and that if they had not found the seashore, it would have been impossible for them ever to return to the fleet.

We left this island eight days after we had arrived there. Then, the next day at noon, we saw another island, not very large, which was about twelve leagues from the first, but most of the first day after leaving we were becalmed. We went close to the coast of this island, and the Indian women whom we carried with us said that it was not inhabited, for those of Caribe had depopulated it, and for this reason we did not stop there. Then that afternoon we saw another; that night, near this island, we found some shoals, for fear of which we anchored, as we did not dare go on until daylight. Then, in the morning, another very large island came into view. We did not go to any of these,[7] in order to better help those who had been left in Hispaniola, and it did not please God, as will appear below.

On the next day at the hour of eating, we reached another island, and it appeared very good to us, for it seemed to be well populated, judging from the many signs of cultivation there.[8] We went and put into a harbor on the coast; the Admiral then ordered a well-manned boat to put ashore to find out what people they were, and also because we needed information about the route, despite the fact that the Admiral, although he had never followed that route, was very much on course, as it turned out. But because uncertainties must always be examined with all possible care, he wanted to have communication there. Some of the men from the boat jumped on shore and went by land to a village, where the people had already gone into hiding. They captured there five or six women and some boys, of whom most were from the prisoners, as on the other island, for these people [the captors] were also of the *caribes*, as we already knew from

7. Montserrat, Redonda, and Antigua.
8. Nevis.

the account of the women whom we brought with us. When this boat was on the point of returning to the ships with the captives, a canoe from a place along the coast approached in which there were four men and two women and a boy, and as soon as they saw the fleet they were so dumbfounded with amazement that for a full hour they sat there without moving from a position about two lombard shots from the ships. During this time, they were seen by those who were in the boat and even by the whole fleet. Then those in the boat went toward them, so close to the shore that, what with their fascination, wondering and thinking what thing this could be, they never saw them until they were close to them, so that they could not do much to escape, although they tried hard to do so; but our men closed so quickly that they could not get away. The *caribes*, when they saw that flight was useless, with great daring took up their bows, the women as well as the men, and I say with great daring because they were only four men and two women and our men were more than twenty-five, of whom they wounded two, one they hit twice in the chest with arrows and the other once in the side, and if it had not been for the fact that the sailors carried oval shields and targets and that they came near them with the boat and overturned their canoe, they would have wounded most of them with their arrows. And after their canoe was overturned, they stayed in the water swimming and sometimes standing, as there were some shallows there, and they [the sailors] had great difficulty in taking them, for they still shot as much as they could, and with all this, there was one whom they could not take until he was badly wounded with a spear thrust from which he eventually died and whom they brought, wounded, to the ships.

The difference in dress between these and the other Indians is that those of Caribe wear their hair very long; the others have it cut irregularly and their heads marked in a hundred thousand different ways, with crosses and other drawings of different kinds, which are done with sharpened reeds, each as he pleases. All of them, those of Caribe and the others, are beardless, so you will very seldom find a man with one. These *caribes* they captured there had their eyes and eyebrows stained, which I think they do for show, and so appear more frightening. One of them says that in one of their islands, called Cayre, which is the first one we saw and to which we did not go, there is much gold: that they go there with nails and steel tools to trade, and that they bring away as much gold as they like.

Later on that day we left this island, where we could not have been more than six or seven hours, and went toward another land which came into sight and which was on the route that we had to follow. We approached it at night. Next day in the morning we went along the coast; there was a lot of land, although it was not very continuous, as there were more than forty odd islets.[9] The land was very high and most of it bare, which was not the case with any other, either those we had seen before or those we have seen since. The land seemed of the kind that would have metals in it. We did not land here, except that a lateen-rigged caravel went to one of these islets, on which they [the crew] found some fishermen's houses. The Indian women we brought with us said that they were not inhabited. We went along this coast for most of this day, until on the following day in the afternoon we came in sight of another island, called Burequen,[10] whose coast we ran for a whole day. It was judged that its length that side was thirty leagues. This island is very beautiful and seems very fertile: those of Caribe come here to make conquests, and carry away many people. These people have no *fustas* and do not know how to go by sea, but according to what these *caribes* we have taken say, they use bows as they [the *caribes*] do, and if by chance they are able to capture those who come to raid them, they also eat them, just as those of Caribe do them. We were two days in a harbor on this island, where many men went ashore, but we were never able to communicate because they all fled like people terrified of the *caribes*. . . .

9. Virgin Islands.
10. Puerto Rico.

Document 3

Writings of Friar Roman on the Antiquities of the Indians,
Which He Collected on Request of the Admiral with Diligence,
as a Man Who Knows Their Language (ca. 1498)

I, Friar Roman,[1] poor hermit of the Order of Saint Geronimo, on
request of the illustrious master the Admiral, Viceroy and Governor
of the islands and mainland of the Indies, write what I have been
able to learn and to know of the beliefs and idolatry of the Indians,
and how they abide by their gods. I will deal with this in the present
writings.[2]

Each one observes a particular mode and superstition in adoring
the idols they keep at home, which they call *cemini*.[3] They believe
that he is like an immortal in heaven, and that no one can see him,
and that he has a mother, and that he has no beginning, and this
they call Iocahuuague Maocoron,[4] and they call his mother Atabei,

---

1. I have accepted the common Hispanic version of the Italian form of Pané's
name, "Roman Pane," which is what appears in Alfonso de Ulloa's transcription of the
lost original text. Similarly, at the head of this document I have translated the full title
from Ulloa's transcription, while in the introduction to the book I have referred to the
work simply as *Antiquities*.

2. Pané sailed on the second voyage of Columbus in September 1493 and was
instructed to reside with King Mayobanex from early 1494, and then King Guarionex
from the beginning of 1495. Internal evidence suggests that the manuscript was not
finished until 1498.

3. Usually now written as *zemi* or *cimi*. "When they are about to go into battle,
they tie small images representing little demons upon their foreheads, for which reason these figures . . . are tied round with strings" (Martyr 1912, dec. 1, bk. 9). Las Casas
also says that they were fitted with speaking tubes (tubes through which their bearers
would speak, so that the figures seemed to be speaking) (1909, chap. 120), probably to
be used for ceremonial oratory.

4. All proper names have been left as they appear in the printed Italian version,
except where inconsistency or error in transcription would obscure etymological connections. Inconsistencies of spelling have not been corrected.

Fig. 1 Funerary *cimi*, Dominican Republic. Shell, cotton, and human skull. Museum of Anthropology, University of Turin. Drawing by Penny Slinger-Hills. (See also Bercht et al. 1997, fig. 82.)

Iermaoguacar, Apito, and Zuimaco, which are five names. Those I am writing about are of the island of Hispaniola; that means that I do not know anything of the other islands, since I have never seen them. In the same way, they know where they came from, and where the sun and the moon originated from, and how the sea was made, and where the dead people go. And they believe that the dead people appear to them in the streets when someone walks alone; therefore, when many go together the dead people do not appear. The people of the past have made them believe all this, as they do not know how to read or count past ten.

I. Where the Indians came from and how

Hispaniola has a province called Coanau, where there is a mountain called Canta,[5] in which there are two caves, one called Cacibagiagua and the other Amaiaua. The majority of the people who populated the island came out of Cacibagiagua.[6] When they were the people of those caves, they would set guard at night, for which a man called Marocael was responsible; one time Marocael lingered at the entrance, [and] they say the sun took him away. Seeing that the sun had taken him away for not keeping guard well, they closed the door; so he was turned into a stone beside the door. Then they also say that others, who had gone fishing, were taken by the sun and became trees, called by them *iobi*, or in a different way *mirabolani*.[7]

The reason why Marocael watched and guarded was in order to see in what places he wanted to send or divide the people; and it seems that he lingered to his own misfortune.

5. "Cauta" in other sources; a cosmological location, as was Matinino, mentioned below. Such places were materially manifested through ritual action and ceremony in the landscape of Antillean caves and mountains, where many archaeological sites are to be found.

6. Caves are highly important in Aiti mythology and ceremonial practice, the name Cacibagiagua recalls the *jagua* tree, source of *genipap*, a magical black dye used as body paint and for protection against malevolent spirits throughout South America. See also Stevens-Arroyo (1988).

7. The hog plum or myrobalan (*Spondias lutea*).

II. How men were separated from women

It happened that a man called Guagugiona told another man, called Giahuuaua,[8] to go pick an herb, called *digo*,[9] that they use to clean their body with when they wash themselves. Giahuuaua left before dawn, but the sun caught him on the way and he became a bird that sings in the morning, like the nightingale, called Giahuha Bagiael.[10] Guagugiona, seeing that the man he sent to pick the *digo* did not come back, decided to come out of the cave called Cacibagiagua.

III

Angry, he decided to leave Cacibagiagua; seeing that those he had sent to pick the *digo* for washing [themselves] were not returning, he told the women, "Leave your husbands and let us go to other lands, and we will obtain great delights.[11] Leave your children, and let us only take with us the herbs [*digo*], then we shall come back for them."

IV

Guagugiona left with the women and went looking for other lands, and he arrived at Matinino, where he immediately left the women

8. The name appears as "Siadruuaua" in the printed Italian version, but this seems an error in transcription of "s" for "g" and "dr" for "h."

9. The identity of this plant is uncertain, although Arrom (in Pané 1988, 178) suggests that it was coca (following Las Casas 1909, chap. 167), despite the usage suggested in this passage.

10. Meaning the descendant of Giahuuaua. This is probably the gray catbird (*Dumetella carolinensis*). "On every anniversary of his transformation he fills the night air with songs, bewailing his misfortunes and imploring his master Vagoniona to come to his help. Such is the explanation they give for the nightingale's song" (Martyr 1912, dec. 1, bk. 9).

11. The original Italian term *gioie* could also mean jewels or ornaments, but given the mention in the subsequent sentence of "herbs," it may be that this was an erroneous transcription of a plant term given in chapter XVII, *gueio*, which is a salt-like tobacco additive made from the riverweed *Mourera fluviatilis* (Arrom 2000, 23n10), termed *kawai* or *weya* in the Guayana region. See Wilbert (1987, 16–17) for analysis of Caribbean tobacco usage in the context of shamanism more widely.

and went to another region, called Guanin,[12] and they had left the
small children by a creek. Then, when hunger started to bother them,
they [the Indians] say they cried and called their mothers who had
left, and their father could not do anything about the children, [who
were] calling with hunger to their mothers, saying *ma ma*, so to
speak, but really asking for the breast. And crying like this and asking for the breast, saying *too, too*, like someone who asks for something with great longing and very slowly, they were transformed
into small animals, like frogs, which are called *tona*, for asking for the
breast, and in this way all the men remained without the women.[13]

V

[They say] that later on women went there again from the said
island of Hispaniola, which before was called Aiti, and that is how
its inhabitants are called; and that one and other islands are called
Bouhi.[14] And since they do not have writings or letters, and cannot give a good account of how they came to know this from their
ancestors, therefore they are not consistent in what they say; nor it
is possible to write in an orderly way what they tell. When Guahagiona [Guagugiona], the man who was taking away all the women,
departed, he also took away the women of his *cacique*, who was called
Anacacugia, deceiving him like he deceived the others, and the more
so a brother-in-law of Guahagiona, Anacacuia, who was traveling
with him on the sea. And being in the canoe,[15] Guahagiona said to his

12. *Guanin* is also a term meaning objects of a gold-copper alloy, for which this
location was the source, as the text indicates at the end of chapter V. Matinino likewise
becomes a source for legends of "Amazon" women, and important thematic ideas are
established between gold and women. See also Steverlynck (2008) and Ralegh (1997,
60–91).

13. "It is for this reason that in the springtime the frogs make these sounds, and
it is also the reason why men alone are frequently found in the caverns of Hispaniola,
and not women" (Martyr 1912, dec. 1, bk. 9).

14. Las Casas (1909, chap. 197) suggests that *Aiti* is a toponym alluding to the
mountainous nature of the island. In the language of the *caribes* of Dominica the
island of Marie-Galante was similarly named *Aichi*; Dominica itself was named *Waita-
kabuli*, literally "she who is tall," in reference to the lofty mountains of the island
easily seen from offshore.

15. The word "canoe" itself derives from the indigenous term *canoa*, which Pané
uses.

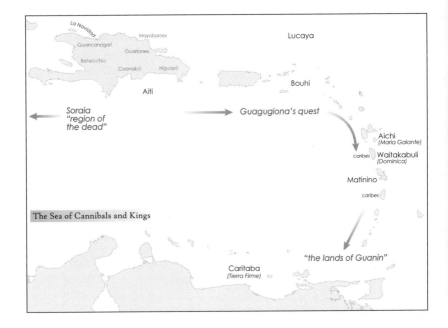

brother-in-law: "look what a nice *cobo* is in the water," the *cobo* being the sea snail.[16] And as he looked in the water to see the *cobo*, Guahagiona took his brother-in-law by the feet and threw him in the sea; so he took all the women for himself,[17] leaving them in Matanino, where they say there are only women nowadays, and he went to another island, called Guanin, and it was called this for what he got when he went there.[18]

VI. Guahagiona went back to the said Canta, where he had taken the women

They say that returning to land, Guahagiona saw that he had left a woman in the sea, and they say that he took great pleasure from her,

16. Snail shell was formed into disks and strung into lengths. Known as *quiriquiripa* on the mainland, it was used a medium of barter and trade (Whitehead 1988, 54–55, 81).

17. The theme of betrayal by a brother or brother-in-law is frequent in origin myths of the region (see Whitehead 2002b, 98–104).

18. *Guanin* means "gold work." These items of gold alloy and carved greenstone are well known from the archaeological record of South America. *Guanin* is also related to the place-name "Guayana" (see Whitehead 1990; 1996).

and right away he looked for pools where he could bathe himself, as he was full of those boils that we call "French disease."[19] Thus, she put him in a *guanara*, which means "secluded place"; and then, staying there, he recovered from the boils. Then she asked him permission to depart, which he granted. That woman was called Guabonito; and from then on Guahagiona changed his name to Biberoci[20] Guahagiona. And the woman Guabonito gave Biberoci Guahagiona many *guanini* and many *cibe* to carry tied to his arms; in those countries the *colecibi* [beads] are made of stones that look very much like marble, and they carry them tied to the arm and neck, and they carry the *guanini* at the ears, making holes when they are little [children], and they are made of metal almost like a coin. They say that the origin of these *guanini* was Guabonito, Albeborael Guahagiona and the father of Albeborael. Guahagiona remained in the land with his father, who was called Hiauna. On the father's side his son was called Hia Guaili Guanin, which means son of Hiauna; therefore, from then on it was called Guanin, and that is how it is called today. And since they have neither letters nor writings, they do not know how to tell these stories well, nor can I write them well. Hence I believe that I will put first what should be last, and will put what is last first. But all that I write in this way is narrated by them just as I write it, and thus I note it down as I have heard it from the peoples of the country.

VII. How women of the island called Aiti, now called Hispaniola, were again

I say that one day men went washing themselves; and, being in the water, it was raining much, and they were longing to have some women, and that several times, when it was raining, they had gone searching for the footprints of their women, without being able to find any news of them, but that day, while they were washing themselves, they saw coming down from some trees, lowering down along the branches, certain shapes of persons, which were neither men nor women, neither had they masculine or feminine characteristics;

19. Not to be identified with syphilis, as the syphilis spirochete did not exist at this time, being produced through contact between an existing New World disease, as described here, and the precursor to syphilis in Europe, the (nonfatal) "French disease" (Harper et al. 2008).

20. Error in transcription for "Albeborael," as his name appears below.

which they went to capture; but they escaped, as if they were eels. Since they could not catch them, they called two or three men, by order of their *cacique*, to go and see how many there were and seek out for each one of them a *caracaracol* man, because they have coarse hands; so they could hold them tight. They said to the *cacique* that there were four of them; and so they brought in four *caracaracoli* men; said *caracaracoli* is a disease, like scabies, that makes the body very coarse. After they caught them, they deliberated on how to make them women, since they had neither a male nor female nature.

VIII. How they made women for themselves

They went looking for a bird called *inriri*, in the past called *inrire cahuuauial*,[21] that makes holes in the trees, known in our language as woodpecker. Likewise, they took those women with neither male nor female nature, and tied their hands and feet, and got the afore-said bird, and tied it to their body [*sic*], and thinking they were wood beams it started its usual work, pecking and puncturing in the place where it usually happens that the nature of women is. In this way, then, the Indians say they got women, according to what the elders tell. Given that I wrote quickly, and I that I did not have enough paper, I could not put in the right place what by mistake I moved to another place. But with all this I am not mistaken, because they believe everything as it is written. Let us now return to what we should have put first, namely their opinion on the origin and beginning of the sea.

IX. How they say the sea was made

There was a man called Giaia, whose real name they do not know; and his son was called Giaiael, which means "child of Giaia": since Giaiael wanted to kill his father, he exiled him, and he was banished for four months; then his father killed him and put his bones in a gourd and hung it to the roof of his home, where it hung for some time. It happened that one day, wishing to see his son, Giaia told his wife: "I want

---

21. A name related to that of the bird, Giahuha Bagiael, ancestor of the nightin-gales, in chapter II.

to see our son Giaiael," and she was happy about it, and taking the gourd she turned it over to see the bones of her son: many large and small fishes came out, and so, seeing that the bones had turned into fish, they decided to eat them.[22] Well now, they say that one day while Gaia had gone to his *conichi*, which means his "domain,"[23] which were inherited, four sons of a woman called Itiba Tahuuaua came, all of one womb and identical;[24] as the woman had died in childbirth, they had opened her up and pulled out the four children; the first they pulled out was called Caracaracoli, which means scabby, and this Caracaracoli was named [omission]; the others had no name.

X. How the four identical children of Itiba Tahuuaua, who died in childbirth, went meddling with the gourd of Giaia, in which his son Giaiael was, who had turned into fish, and none of them dared to snatch it, except for Dimiuan Caracaracol, who grabbed it; and all ate their fill of fish

And while they ate, they heard Giaia coming back from his gardens, and quickly trying to hang the gourd back up, they did not hang it properly, so the gourd fell down and broke. They say that so much water came out of the gourd that it filled the whole world, and with that many fish came out; therefore they believe it gave rise to the sea. Then they left that place and found a man, whom they called Conel, who was mute.

XI. Of the things that the four brothers went through when they left fleeing from Giaia

As they arrived at the door of Bassamanaco, and they heard that he had *cazzabí* [cassava], they said, "*Ahiacauo Guarocoel,*" which means

22. This mythological act of ancestral anthropophagy suggests that the *caribes* were not unique in their supposed cannibalism and were in fact culturally similar to the people of Aiti. However, a similar funerary treatment was adduced in the case of the *caribes* to be indicative of cannibalism (see the account of Diego Chanca). Las Casas also says that the bones of the dead were placed inside wooden *cimis* that took the name of the deceased (1909, chap. 120).

23. *Conichi* is equivalent to an indigenous word taken into Spanish, *conuco,* a small farm or garden.

24. *Gemelli* in the printed Italian, literally meaning "twins."

"We know this grandfather of ours." Seeing that his brothers were going ahead, Deminan Caracaracol went in to see if he could have some *cazzabí;* said *cazzabí* is the bread that people eat in that country.[25] Walking inside Aiamanaco's[26] house, Caracaracol asked him for *cazzabí,* the aforesaid bread, and he put a hand to his nose and hit him on the shoulder with a *guanguaio;*[27] the *guanguaio* was full of *cagioba*[28] that he had prepared that day; the *cagioba* is a certain powder, which they take as a purgative or for other effects that you will learn of later on. They take it with a cane half an arm long, putting one end in the nose and the other in the powder; and so they draw it in with the nose, and this purges them greatly. And so he gave him that *guanguaio* instead of the bread he had made; and he left very angry because they had asked him to leave. . . . After that, Caracaracol went to his brothers and told them what had happened to him with Baiamanicoel, and the *guanguaio* he had been hit with on the shoulder, which was hurting a lot. So his brothers checked his shoulder; and they saw that it was swollen. And it kept swelling to the point that he was close to death. So they tried to cut it open, but they could not; and taking a stone axe, they opened it, and a live turtle came out, female; and so they built their house and raised the turtle. I have not heard anything else about this, and what I wrote is of little use. Moreover, they say that the sun and the moon came out from a cave that lies in the country of a *cacique,* called Maucia Tiuuel; said cave is called Giououaua, and they hold it in great esteem, and they paint it all over in their own way, without any human figure, with many leaves and similar things. And in said cave there were two *cimini* made of stone, half an arm big, with the hands tied, and they looked as if they were sweating; and they had them in great esteem; and when there was drought they say that they went to visit them in the cave, and it rained at once. And of said *cimini* one is called Boinaiol and the other Maroia.

25. See Documents 1a and 1B, note 16.
26. This name also appears as Bassamanaco, Baiamanicoel, and Gamanacoal in the text.
27. A gob of sputum, spit, or phlegm.
28. This term appears in other sources as *cohoba,* a tobacco-based drug that was central to ritual and the performance of authority among the caciques. Seeds of *Anadenanthera peregrina* (previously known as *Piptadenia peregrina*) were ground and added to dried tobacco. This snuff is still used in Amazonia and coastal Venezuela, where it is known as *niopoi* (*ñopo*).

XII. Of what they feel about the wandering around of the dead, and what they are like, and what they do

They believe there is a place where the dead go, called Coaibai, which lies in a part of an island called Soraia.[29] The first who stayed in Coaibai they say was called Machetaurie Guaiaua, who was the lord of the said Coaibai, residence and house of the dead.

XIII. Of the form they say the dead take

They say that during the day they are shut in and at night they walk around, and that they eat a certain fruit, called *guabazza*,[30] which tastes like . . . and that during the day they are . . . and at night they would turn into fruit, and they feast, and go with the living. And to recognize them they follow this way: they touch their belly, and if they do not find the belly button, they say that it is *operito*, which means "dead"; therefore they say that the dead have no belly button; and so, not checking on that, they were deceived a few times; and they lay with one of the women of Comboi [Coaibai], and when they think they are embracing them, they have nothing; they disappear. This is what they believe until these days. In a living person, they call the spirit *goeiz*, and after death they call it *opia*;[31] which *goeiz* they say often appears in form of either men or women; and they say that when a man wanted to fight with it, when he came to blows, it disappeared, and the man ended up holding some trees and hanging from them. And this is the belief they share, children and adults; and that it appears to them in the form of a father or mother, or brothers, or relatives, and in other shapes. The fruit they say the dead eat is as big as a quince. And the aforesaid dead do not appear to them by day, but always at night; so it is with great fear that someone dares to walk alone at night.

29. I.e., to the west, region of death and disappearance.
30. The guava fruit.
31. The terms *opia* and *operito* and the association here with death and resurrection suggest connections with obeah magic, a form of vodou. See note 38 in the introduction and Whitehead (2002b, 49).

XIV. Where they get this from, and who keeps them in such belief

There are certain men who associate among themselves, and they are called *bohuti*,[32] who make many tricks, as we shall explain later, to make them [the people] believe that they talk with them [the dead], and know all their deeds and secrets, and that when they are ill they take the illness away, and so they deceive them. I have seen parts of this with my own eyes, while of the other things I narrate only what I learned from many, especially the principal men, with whom I associated more than with others, since they believe these tales more certainly than the others: because, like the Moors, they have their law reduced to ancient songs, by way of which they rule themselves, as the Moors by way of writing. And when they want to sing their songs, they play a certain instrument, called *maiohauau*, made of wood and concave, made strong and very thin, one arm long and half an arm wide; and the side which is played is shaped like a blacksmith's tongs, and the other side is similar to a club; so it looks like a gourd, with a long neck; and they play this instrument, which has so much voice that it can be heard a league[33] and a half away. To that sound they sing the songs that they learn by heart; and the most important men play it, who learn how to play it and sing with it as children, according to their custom.[34] Let us now go on and deal with many things about other ceremonies and customs of the Gentiles.

*XV. Of the observations of these **buhuitihu** [bohuti] Indians, and how they practice medicine, and teach to the people; and in their medicinal cures they are often wrong*

All, and the majority of those of the island of Hispaniola, have many *cimini* of various kinds. Some hold the bones of the father, or of the mother, or of the relatives, or of the forebears; and they are made of stone or wood. And of the two kinds they have many: some that speak, others that make food grow, others that make rain, and others that make winds blow; those simple, ignorant people believe those

32. Shaman. Las Casas uses the form *bohique*.
33. League: see Documents 1a and 1b, note 2.
34. Called also *areyto*, these songs were indeed a historical and cosmological archive.

Fig. 2 Shamanic spectacles, Puerto Rico. Carved bone. Museum of the University of Puerto Rico, catalog # 12-711. Drawing by Penny Slinger-Hills.

idols do these things, or to speak more properly, those demons, since they have no knowledge of our holy faith. When someone is ill, they bring him the aforesaid *buhuitihu* doctor. [. . .] He must purge himself like the ill person; and to purge himself he takes a certain powder called *cohoba*, inhaling it by the nose, which intoxicates him in such a way that they do not know what they do; and they say many things out of the ordinary, in which they affirm that they talk with the *cimini,* and that they tell them [the *cimini*] that the illness came from them.

XVI. Of what the said **buhuitihu** do

When they go to visit a patient, before they leave their homes they take from the pots some lampblack or crushed charcoal, and they blacken their whole face, to make the patient believe whatever they want about his illness, and then they take some tiny bones and some flesh; and wrapping all this with something so that it does not fall out, they put it in [the *buhuitihu*'s] mouth, the patient already having been purged with the powder we mentioned. As the doctor walks into the house of the patient, he sits down, and everybody falls silent; and if there are children they are sent outside, so that do not get in the way of the *buhuitihu* in his work; only one or two of the most important men remain in the house. When they are alone, they take some herbs of the *gioia*[35] . . . long, and another herb folded in an onion leaf, half a quart[36] long, and the said *gioia* is the one that

35. Given as *gueio* below; see also note 11 above.
36. A half-quart is approximately twenty-nine cubic inches.

Fig. 3 *Cohoba* mortar, Dominican Republic. Ironwood. Metropolitan Museum, New York, the Michael R. Rockefeller Memorial Collection. Drawing by Penny Slinger-Hills.

everybody commonly takes, and having ground them with their hands they knead them; and then they put them in their mouth at night, to vomit what they have eaten, so that it does not harm them. And then they start producing the aforesaid song; and lighting a torch they take that juice. The *buhuitihu* does that first, and having waited a while, he stands up and goes toward the patient, who as I said sits alone in the middle of the house, and then he faces him and takes him by the legs, [and] manipulating his upper legs runs down to the feet; then he pulls him hard, as if he wants to extract something; then he goes to the door and closes it, and talks, saying: "Go away to the mountain or to the sea or wherever you want"; and with a puff of breath, like someone who is blowing chaff, goes back and joins his hands and closes his mouth, and the hands shiver as when one is feeling cold, and he blows on the hands and sucks in, as when sucking bone marrow, and he sucks the patient on the neck, or the stomach, or the shoulders, or the cheeks, or the breast, or the belly, or many parts of the body. With this done, they start coughing and making faces as if they had eaten something bitter, and he spits out on his hand the thing we mentioned, which in his house or on the way he had put in his mouth; either rock, or bone, or flesh, as we said. And if it is food, he says to the patient: "Know that you have eaten something that caused the illness you suffer; see how I extracted it from the body, where the *cemi* had put it because you do not pray to him, or build him a temple, or offer him any goods." And if it is made of stone he says: "Keep it well." And sometimes they are convinced that those stones are good, and are useful to make women deliver, and they keep them with great care, wrapped in cottonwood, in some tiny baskets, and they feed them with the same food they eat; as they do with the *cimini* that they keep in the house.[37] On ceremonial days, they bring much food, fish, meat, bread, and whatever food they want, and put all these offerings in the house of the *cimiche* for the idol to eat. The following day, after the *cimiche* have eaten, they take all the food home. God help them, because the *cimiche* cannot eat that or other things, the *cimiche* being a dead thing made of stone or wood.

37. This description of shamanic curing and divination is highly accurate and completely consistent with modern ethnographic accounts from across South America and the Caribbean.

XVII. How sometimes the aforesaid doctors were wrong

If after they [the *buhuitihu*] have done the aforesaid things and the
patient then dies anyway, if the dead person has many relatives, that
is, if he is a lord of a manor, and can stand up to the said *buhuitihu*
(which means doctor), since those who cannot do not dare to chal-
lenge these doctors, then the one who wants revenge does this:
wanting to know if the patient died because of the doctor, or because
he may not have followed the prescription as he was ordered, then
they take a herb, which is called *gueio* and has leaves similar to
those of the basil, big and wide, and with a different name it is called
zachon.[38] So they take the juice of the leaves and cut the nails and
the hair bangs of the dead person and they pulverize them with two
stones and mix them with the juice of the said herb, and they give
it to the dead person to drink through the nose or the mouth; and
while they do this they ask the dead person if the doctor was the
cause of his death and if he followed the prescription. And they ask
this several times, until the dead person speaks as if he were alive; in
such a way he answers all that they want to know from him, saying that the *buhuitihu* did not follow the diet, or on that occasion
was responsible for his death; and they say that the doctor asks him
if he is alive, and how it is that he speaks so clearly; and he answers
that he is dead. And having known what they wanted to know, they
return him to the grave, from where they took him, to know from
him what we just said.[39] They do their magic in a different way, to
know what they want: they take the dead, and they make a bonfire,
similar to that with which the charcoal burner makes charcoal, and
when the firewood has turned into embers, they throw the dead body
onto that fierce glow, and they cover it with earth, like the charcoal
burner covers the charcoal, and they leave it there as long as they
want; and keeping the dead person in that way, they question him,
as it was mentioned of the other, who may answer that he does not
know anything; and so they question him ten times, after which he
does not speak anymore. They ask him if he is dead; but he does not
speak more than ten times.

38. See note 11 above.
39. See introduction for a discussion of how this necromancy relates to the
"zombi" complex and of how, in this chapter, the use of snakes relates to the vodou
snake deity Dumbala, as well as indigenous assault sorcery; see also Whitehead (2002b,
125–26).

XVIII. How the relatives of the dead take revenge, because they got an answer through the magic of the brew

One day the relatives of the dead person may get together and wait for the aforesaid *buhuitihu*, and they beat him up, break his legs and arms and head, so they smash him all up, and they leave him there, thinking that they have killed him. And at night they say that many snakes of various kinds come, white, black, and green, and of many other colors, which lick the face and the whole body of the aforesaid doctor, who, as we said, was thought dead and left there; and he stays there two or three nights; and they say that while he stays there, the bones of the legs and arms join again and heal, and that he stands up and walks slowly and goes back home; and those who see him question him, saying, "Were you dead?" but he answers that the *cimini* came to help him in the form of snakes. And the relatives of the dead, angry because they thought they had avenged the death of their relative, seeing that he is alive again, they get upset, and try to lay hands on him to kill him; and if they can catch him, they rip his eyes out, and they crush his testicles; because they say that none of these doctors can be killed, however violently he is attacked, if his testicles are not torn off.[40]

How they learn what they want from the one they burn, and how they revenge him

When they uncover the fire, the escaping smoke rises up high as far as the eye can see, making a screeching sound as it exits the fire pit. Then it comes back again and enters the doctor *buhuitihu*'s house, and immediately he falls ill, and anyone else who did not obey the prescription, and he breaks out in ulcers and he peels all over the body; and so they get the sign that he did not provide good care, and that's why the patient died. Therefore they try to kill him, as it was already said of the other. These are the magic spells they customarily do.

40. The ritual skills of autogenesis and symbiogenesis (being and becoming) are central to effective shamanic action and vision; the killing of a shaman thus requires elaborate and violent ritual procedures to deconstruct that power (see Whitehead 2002b, 150–51).

XIX. *How they make and keep the stone and wood* cimini

Those made of stone [*sic*] are made this way. Someone is walking
along and says that he sees some tree which moves at the roots: and
the man stops with great fear, and asks him who he is. And he replies:
"I am *bihuitihu,* and this tells you who I am." And the man goes to
the aforesaid doctor and tells him what he saw; and the sorcerer or
witch doctor rushes to see the tree of which the other told him, and
he sits next to it, and he does *cagioba* to it, as we said before in the
tale of the four brothers. Having done the *cagioba,* he stands up and
calls to it with honorifics, like to a mighty lord, and he asks it: "Tell
me who you are, and what you are doing here, and what you want
from me, and why you sent for me. Tell me if you want met to cut
you, or if you want to come with me, and how do you want me to
carry you, and I will build you a house with possessions." So that
tree, or *cimiche,* made idol, or devil, answers, telling him the form in
which he wants to be made. And he cuts it, and makes it in the way
he [the *cimiche*] ordered him; he builds his house with its garden,
and many times a year he does him *cagioba;* said *cagioba* is to give
him prayers, or to please him, and to ask him good or bad things, and
also to ask him for wealth. And when they want to know if they will
win a victory against their enemies, they go into a house in which
only the most important men go; and their lord is the first to do
cagioba, and he plays [*maiohauau*]; and while he does the *cagioba,*
none of those who are in the gathering make judgment until the lord
is done. But as he ends his prayer, he stays for quite a long time with
his head hung down and arms lying over his knees; then he raises his
head and looks toward the sky and speaks. Then all reply in turn in
a loud voice; and after they all have spoken, they give thanks, and he
narrates the vision he had, drunk with *cagioba,* which he had taken
by the nose and which rose up in his head; and he says he talked
with the *cimi* and that they will win a victory, or their enemies will
flee, or there will be many casualties, or war, or famine, or similar
things, along with what comes into his mind, who's drunk. Consider
the state of his brain; hence they say they think they see the houses
turning upside down and the men walking with their feet turned
toward the sky. And this *cagioba* they use for the stone and wood
cimini, as with the dead bodies, as we said earlier.

The stone *cimini* are of diverse kinds. There are some that they say the doctors take out of their bodies; patients like to have those since they are the best for making pregnant women deliver. There are others that speak, which are shaped like a big turnip with the leaves lying on the ground, and as long as those of the caper; their leaves are generally shaped like the elm leaf; and others have three tips, and they say that these make the yucca produce.[41] They have roots similar to a turnip. The leaf of the yucca has generally six or seven tips; I do not know what I should compare it to, since it does not look like anything I have seen in Spain or other countries. The stalk is as tall as a man.

Let us now tell of the belief they have about the idols and the *cimini,* and of the great deceptions they use them for.

*XX. Of the **cimi** Bugia and Aiba, which, they say, was burned by them when there were wars, and then when he was washed with the juice of the yucca, his arms grew, and his eyes came out again, and his body grew up*

The yucca was small, and with the aforesaid water and juice they washed it to make it grow; and they affirm that it caused diseases to those who had made said *cimi,* for not having given him some yucca to eat. Said *cimi* was called Baidrama. And when someone fell ill, they called the *buhuitiú* and asked him what was the cause of his disease, and he answered that Badriama had sent it, because he did not feed those who were taking care of his house. And the *bihutiú* said that the *cimi* Baidrama had told him that.

*XXI. Of the **cimi** of Guamorete*

They say that when they built the house of Guamorete, who was a chief, they put on top of his house a *cimi* called Corocote. So they say that it got up and went by some creek at a distance of a crossbow shot

41. There are numerous archaeological examples of these tripointed stones. For broader discussions of these stones as well as other *cimi* forms and how their "personality" or character was understood and revealed through making them (as described in this chapter), see Oliver (2009, 59–68) and Santos-Granero (2009).

Fig. 4 Tripointed fertility *cimi*, Dominican Republic. Fossiliferous stone. Metropolitan Museum, New York. Drawing by Penny Slinger-Hills.

from there. And they say that at night it would come down to sleep with the women, and that after Guamorete died, another *cacique* got hold of the *cimi* while it was still sleeping with the women. Moreover, they say that two *corone*[42] grew up on its head, so they were saying: "Since it has two *corone*, it must be the son of Corocote." And they held this for sure. Then another *cacique*, called Guatabanex, had this *cimi*, and his place was called Giacaba.

XXII. Of another **cimi**, called Opigielguouiran, held by a chief called Cauauaniouaua, who had many subjects under him

Said Opigielguouiran, they say, has four legs like a dog, and it is made of wood,[43] and at night it often went outside into the forest. They would seek it, and take it back home, and tie it with ropes, but it would go back to the forest. And they say that when the Christians arrived in the island Hispaniola, it fled and went in a lagoon, and they followed its tracks there; but they do not see it anymore, and know nothing of it. As I bought it, I am selling it.

XXIII. Of another **cimi**, called Guabancex

This *cimi* Guabancex was in the country of a great *cacique*, one of the most important ones, called Aumatex, and said *cimi* was a woman, and they say that there are two others who accompany her: one is the harbinger, and the other the gatherer and governor of the waters. And when Guabancex becomes upset, they say that [it, she] moves the wind, and the water, and blows things down, and uproots the trees. This *cimi* they say is female, and is made of the stones of that country, and the other two *cimini* that accompany her are called Guatauuna, that is, summoners, who by order of Guabancex call the other *cimini* of that province to help in making the wind and the water; and another is called Coatrischie,[44] which they say gathers the waters in

42. Italian *corona* = crown; the meaning here is obscure.
43. See figure 6, showing that Pané makes here a very precise description. The first syllable of the name of this *cimi*—*opiy*—can be connected to the ideas of night, sorcery, and death (see notes 31, 40).
44. Similar to Chalchiuhtlicue, sister of the Aztec rain god, Tlaloc; she likewise brought water from the sea to the land through the sky.

Fig. 5 Opigielguouiran *cimi*, Dominican Republic. Wood. Department of Anthropology, Museum of Natural History, Smithsonian Institution, Washington, D.C. Drawing by Penny Slinger-Hills. (See also Bercht et al. 1997, fig. 101.)

the valleys between the mountains and lets them go to destroy the country. And they hold this as a certain truth.

XXIV. *Of what they believe of another* cimi *that is called Faraguuaol*

This *cimi* is of a main *cacique* of the island Hispaniola and it is an idol, and they attribute to him many names, and it was found in the following way. They say that one day, before the island was discovered in past times, they do not know how long ago, while they were hunting they found a certain animal, and they ran after it, and it escaped into a hole in the ground; and while they were looking for it they saw a log that seemed to be alive.[45] Seeing this, the hunter rushed to his lord, who was a *cacique* and the father of Guaraionel, and he told him what he had seen. So they went there, and found that thing as the hunter had said; and taking that trunk they built a house for it. They say that several times it left that house and went back to the place from where they had taken it; not exactly that place, but close by; then the aforesaid lord or his son Guaraionel who had recovered it, found it disguised; and that another time they tied it up and put it in a sack; but in spite of this, all tied up, it would walk like before. And this, those ignorant people hold for utterly certain.

XXV. *Of the things that two main caciques of the island Hispaniola affirm to have said: one named Cazziuaquel, father of the mentioned Guarionel; the other named Gamanacoal*

And that great lord, which they say is in the sky, as it is written in the beginning of this book [Iocahuuague Maocoron], this Caizzihu practiced fasting, which they all habitually do. Thus, they stay in an enclosed space for six or seven days, without eating anything, only the juice of herbs, with which they wash themselves.[46] After that, they start eating some food that nourishes them. And during the time in which they have been without eating, because of the

45. A similar *cimi* was found at Baracoa, Cuba, and is now in the Museo Antropológico Montane, Havana.
46. This is the herb *digo* mentioned above. The reference here to fasting using this herb certainly suggests a coca compound, since coca is an appetite suppressant.

Fig. 6 Faraguuaol *cimí,* Cuba. Wood. Montané Anthropological Museum, University of Havana. Drawing by Penny Slinger-Hills.

weakness they feel in the body and the head they say they have seen things, perhaps desired by them; since they all practice abstinence in honor of their *cimini,* in order to know if they will win a victory against their enemies, or to gain riches, or for whatever thing they desire. And they say that this *cacique* claimed that he had talked with Giocauugama, who told him that those who survived him would enjoy their rule for a short time, because dressed people would arrive in their country, who would dominate and kill them, and that they would starve to death. At first they thought that these people had to be the *cannibali,*[47] but then they considered that since they [the *cannibali*] do not do anything else other than grab and run, it had to be other people that the *cimi* indicated. Hence, they now believe that these are the admiral and the people that he brings.

Now I want to narrate what I saw and went through when other friars and myself were traveling in Castiglia;[48] and I, Friar Roman, poor hermit, remained, and then I went to La Maddalena [Magdalena] to a fortress that Don Christopher Columbus, admiral, viceroy and governor of the islands and the mainland of the Indies, had built, by command of the King Don Fernando and the Queen Donna Isabella, our lords. While I was in that fortress with Artiaga, its captain, by command of Don Christopher Columbus, God wanted to illuminate with the light of the Holy Catholic Faith a whole house of the important people by the aforesaid fortress of La Magdalena, of the province that was formerly called Maroris [Macorix], and its lord is called Guauaouoconel, which means child of Guauaenechin.

In that house his servants and favorites live, whose family name is Giahuuauoriú, and they were sixteen in total, all relatives, among whom there were five brothers. One of them died, and the other four received the water of holy baptism; and I believe that they died martyrs, from what I saw of their death and constancy. The first who received death, or rather the water of the Holy Baptism, was an Indian called Guaticaua, who then got the name of Giovanni. This man was the first Christian, who suffered a cruel death; and it seems to me for sure that he died as a martyr:[49] because I have heard from

47. See discussion of "cannibals" in the introduction.
48. Castile, the dominant kingdom in Spain. Isabella was queen of Castile and Ferdinand king of Aragon.
49. Las Casas explicitly disputes this, saying that they were killed for their allegiance to the Spanish, not for their faith, and that anyway the natives were not intellectually capable of killing for such a reason (1909, chap. 167).

people who witnessed his death, that he was saying: "Dio Aboriadacha, Dio Aboriadacha," which means: I am the servant of God. In
this way his brother Antonio died, and another with him, saying the
same thing. The people of this house all joined to do what I approved.
Those who survived are Christians thanks to the aforementioned
Don Christopher Columbus, viceroy and governor of the Indies; and
nowadays there are many more Christians for the grace of God.

Let us now tell what happened to us in the island of La Magdalena

While I was staying in the aforesaid La Magdalena, the said lord
Admiral came to aid Ariaga and some Christians who were besieged
by the enemies, subjects of a principal *cacique* called Caonabo. At
that time, the lord Admiral told me that the province of La Magdalena Maroris had a language different from the other, and that
its dialect wasn't understood all over the land. So he told me to go
and stay with another important *cacique*, called Guarionex, lord of
many people, where the language was understood all over the land.
So, on his command, I went to stay with the said Guarionex. To tell
the truth, I told the lord governor Don Christopher Columbus: "My
Lord, why does your Excellency want me to stay with Guarionex, if
I do not know a language other than that of Maroris? Your Excellency gave me permission to go with someone from Nuhuirci, people
who then became Christian, and knew both languages." Which he
granted, and he told me to take with me whoever I preferred. And
God in His goodness gave me the best of the Indians as a companion,
and the most informed on the Holy Catholic Faith, and then he took
him away. God be praised, who gave him to me and took him away;
because he truly was like a good son and brother to me; and he was
Guaicauanú, who then became Christian and was called Giovanni.
Of the things that we went through there, I, a poor hermit, will say
some, and how Guaicaunaú and I left and went to Isabella, and there
we waited for the lord Admiral until he came back from aiding the
Magdalena, and as he arrived, we left to go where the lord governor
had sent us in the company of a man called Giovanni of Artiaga, who
was in charge of a fortress that the said governor Don Christopher
Columbus had build half a league from where we were supposed
to stay. And the lord Admiral commanded the aforesaid Giovanni

of Artiaga to supply us with the provisions of the fortress, which is called La Concepción. And so we stayed with that *cacique* Guarionex almost two years, always teaching him our Holy Faith and the customs of the Christians. In the beginning he showed goodwill and gave hope that he would do everything we wanted and become Christian, telling us to teach him the Paternoster, the Ave Maria, and the Credo, and all the other prayers and things that belong to the Christian. And so he learned the Paternoster, the Ave Maria, and the Credo; and so did many of those who lived in his house; and each morning he said his prayers, and had those of his house say them twice a day. But then he grew annoyed and gave up his good intentions because of the other principals [*caciques*] of that land, who reprimanded him for wanting to obey the Christian law; maintaining that the Christians were wicked, and controlled their lands by force. Instead they advised him to stop bothering about anything to do with the Christians, but to come to an agreement, and together conspire to kill them, because they could not please them and had resolved that they did not want under any circumstances to do anything in their fashion. That is why he gave up his good intentions, and as we realized that he was less attentive and was giving up what we had taught him, we decided to leave and go where our efforts in teaching the Indians and training them in the things of the Holy Faith would be more fruitful. And so we went to another principal *cacique* who showed us goodwill, saying that he wanted to be Christian, and he was named Mauiatué.

How we left to go to the country of the said Mauiatué, that is to say, myself, Friar Roman Pane, poor hermit, and Friar Giovan Borgognone of the order of Saint Francis, and Giovan Matteo, the first to receive the water of the Holy Baptism on the island of Hispaniola

The second day after we departed from the settlement and house of Guarionex to go to the other *cacique*, called Mauiatué, the people of Guarionex were building a house near the house of prayer, where we had left some images so that the catechumens would kneel before them and pray and console themselves, who were the mother, brothers, and relatives of Giovan Matteo, the first Christian; seven more joined them; and then all the people of his house became Christians,

and persevered in their good intent, following our faith: so that all
of the aforesaid house kept guard over that house of prayer and
over some garden plots that I had made and I had people look after.
And while they watched over that house, two days after (the second day after) we left for Mauiatué, six men went to the house of
prayer, which the catechumens, who were seven, had under guard,
and by order of Guarionex they told them to take the images that
Fray Roman had left in custody of the aforementioned catechumens
and to smash them and tear them apart, because Fray Roman and
his party had gone away and would not know who had done that.
Thus, when the six servants of Guarionex went there, they found six
children who watched over the house of prayer, fearing exactly what
then happened; the children told them they did not want them to
enter, as they had been told to do; but they entered by force, seized
the images, and took them away.

*XXVI. Of what happened to the images, and of the miracle God did to show
his power*

As they left the house of prayer, they threw the images on the
ground, and they covered them with soil and pissed on them, saying: "Now your fruits will be good and large"; and then they buried
them in a garden, saying that the fruit they planted would have been
good; all this was done as an insult. When the children, who were
watching over the aforementioned house of prayer by order of the
aforementioned catechumens, saw this, they ran to tell the adults,
who were in their farms, that the people of Guarionex had destroyed
and insulted the images. When they heard this, they left what they
were doing and ran yelling to let Don Bartolomeo Columbus know,
who was governing that land on behalf of his brother the Admiral,
who had gone to Castile. As lieutenant of the viceroy and governor
of the islands, he put the wrongdoers on trial, and once the truth
was known he condemned them to be burned at the stake. In spite
of this, Guarionex and his subjects did not give up the evil intent of
killing the Christians on the day set to give them the gold tribute
that they were obliged to pay. But this conspiracy was discovered:
and so they were caught on the same day they had planned to carry

it out. And in spite of all that they persevered in their purpose; and putting it into practice, they killed four men, and Giovan Matteo, the principal Christian,[50] and Antonio, his brothers, who had received the Holy Baptism, and then they ran to where the images were hidden, and they ripped them to pieces. After several days, the owner of that garden went to pick up *agi*, which are roots similar to horseradish; and in the spot where the images had been buried, two or three *agi* had sprouted, as intercrossing each other, in the shape of a cross.[51] It was impossible that anyone else would have discovered such a cross; nevertheless the mother of Guarionex discovered it; she is the worst woman I have known among those groups. She thought it a great miracle, and, God knows why, said to the lord of the fortress of the Conception: "This miracle was revealed by God, in the spot where the images were found."

Now we tell how the first to receive the Holy Baptism became Christians, and how much work it took to make them all Christians

Truly the island is in great need of people to punish the lords when they deserve it, make them understand matters of holy Catholic faith, and train them in that, given that they cannot, and do not know how to, dispute this. I can say that truthfully, given how I have struggled to find this out, as I think was understood from what has been said so far; and a word is enough to the wise.

So the first Christians were the aforementioned of the island of Hispaniola, that is, Giauauuariú, in whose house there were seventeen persons, who all became Christians, just by [his] letting them know that there is one God, who made everything, and created the sky and the earth, with nothing else being argued or explained; given that, they easily believed. But with the others force and ingenuity are necessary, because not everyone is of the same nature: therefore, if they have a good beginning and a better end, there will be others that will start well and then will laugh at what is taught to them; for them force and punishment are necessary.

50. Although the text reads *scrivano,* this seems certainly a mistranscription or mistranslation of *cristiano.*

51. Since it is a root crop, this is the sweet potato, not the *aji* (chili pepper).

The first to receive the Baptism on the island of Hispaniola was Giovan Matteo, who was baptized on the day of Saint Matthew Evangelist[52] in the year 1496, and then his whole house, where many have been Christians. And we would make better progress if there were someone to educate them and teach them the holy Catholic faith, and people to control them. And if someone wants to know why I make this business seem so easy, I reply because I've seen it through experience, especially with a *cacique* called Mahuuiatiuire, who has been displaying goodwill for three years, saying that he wants to be Christian, and that he does not want to have more than one woman; because they usually have two, and three, and the principal men have ten, fifteen, and twenty.

This is what I could understand and find out about the customs and rites of the Indians of Hispaniola, with all the diligence I could. For this I do not claim any profit, neither spiritual nor temporal. Our Lord wish, if this serves his benefit and service, to give me the grace to be able to persevere, and, if it has to be otherwise, to take my intellect away.

The end of the work
of the poor hermit Roman Pane.

---

52. September 21. This discussion by Pané of conversion and martyrdom is also significant in the light of recent work by Consuelo Varela and Isabel Aguirre (2006, 200–3) in recovering little-known texts and testimonies from the period that Pané discusses in this chapter. As Varela and Aguirre show, the issue of conversion of the natives was a matter of conflict among the Spanish, and Christopher Columbus in particular appears to have actively prevented missionary conversion, preferring instead to treat the natives as a potential source of slaves. Notably, this information also undercuts Arrom's efforts to present native and Spanish relationships, as well as the matter of conversion itself, in a positive light, even misinterpreting the above passage about Guarionex's people pissing on and defiling Christian objects (Arrom 1999, 36n155).

Document 4

The Deposition of Rodrigo Figueroa on the
Islands of the Barbarous *Caribes* (1520)

*Judgment of Rodrigo de Figueroa, Resident Magistrate and Judge in the
Audiencia of Santo Domingo, relating that all the islands which are not
inhabited by the Christians, except those of Trinidad, Lucaya, Barbuda, Los
Gigantes, and Margarita, are those of the barbarous **caribe** Indians: in this
year 1520*

By me, the lawyer Rodrigo de Figueroa, judge in residence and senior
justice of this island of Hispaniola, also judge of the Royal Audiencia for appellants in this district, also manager of the *caciques* and
Indians of this island for the Queen and the Emperor, our lords, in
which capacity I have to hand a lot of information about the islands
and the mainland of Tierra Firme, and which Indians and settlements
are those of the *caribes*, and am able to indicate which Indians can be
made Christian and those which can be taken as slaves, this statement
being made as a judicial ruling.

Given the information mentioned above by me and that ancillary
and related information of others, of which they are many on this
island, such as pilots, captains, and sailors, and other persons who are
accustomed to travel to the coast of Tierra Firme and the islands and
other far-off regions and other places discovered in the Ocean Sea
[Atlantic], and also we are likewise able to have information from
religious persons; also I have seen the information given earlier by
the judge Alonso Zuazo, who was also given certain tasks the results
of which I intend to send to Your Majesty.

I declare and rule that all the islands which are not populated by
Christians, except those of Trinidad, Lucaya, Barbuda, Los Gigantes,
and Margarita, are those which are populated by *caribes*, as well as
other barbarous enemies of the Christians, who reject all attempts
to convert them, as do the others who also eat human flesh; and

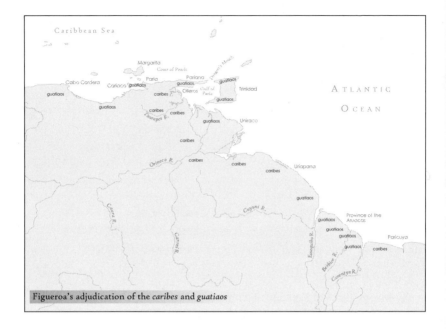

Figueroa's adjudication of the *caribes* and *guatiaos*

they have not sought, or wished to allow, communication with the Christians, including the missionaries of our holy Catholic faith; also concerning Tierra Firme, from what I have come to understand and been able to find out, I am able to say and affirm that much farther down the coast, which stretches from those parts as far as the Coast of Pearls, there is a province called Paracuya,[1] which is inhabited by *guatraos* [= *guatiaos*, allies], and from there, coming by the coast toward the Gulf of Paria, there is another province which stretches as far as that of the Aruacas, which is held by the *caribes*; and coming up the coast from this province there is the said province of the Aruacas, who declare themselves to be *guatraos* and friends of the Christians; and they are worthy to be friends of the Christians and must be very well treated; farther beyond this province, the province of Uriapana [Orinoco], which is declared to belong to the *caribe* enemies of the Christians, who eat human flesh; and farther along the same coast of the Gulf of Paria is another province, called Uniraco, which is judged to belong to *guatraos* and friends of the Christians,

1. Possibly referring to the Palikur of the Atlantic Coast in the region of the Oyapok River, the modern border between Brazil and French Guiana. They were also known to the Portuguese through the 1500 and 1509 voyages of Vicente Yañez Pinzón.

who peacefully trade and communicate with the Christians, and with the other *guatraos*, also friends of the Christians; farther along the coast of the Gulf is another province, through which flows the river Taurapes [Guarapiche]; the Indians of which province are declared also to be *caribes*, and like those *caribes* mentioned above; and even farther along, in the inlet of the Gulf, is another province, called Olleros,[2] and those there are also judged to be *caribes*, along with the province of Macarapana as far as the province of Cariaco, along the same coast, as far as the province of Pariana, where there is another province in the Gulf of Paria, stretching to the Dragon's Mouth;[3] the Indians of Pariana are judged to be *guatraos* and very tractable and friends of the Christians; and within Cariaco, at the entrance point to the province of Cariaco, in the territory of the *cacique* Salzedo, all who are along the coast of *Cariaco*, including those in Covincia, Chirivichi, and Macarapana, as far as the river Unari, along all of the coast, are declared to be *guatraos*, agreeable and very much friends of the Christians; and from this province of Unari farther along the coast to Cabo Cordera and Cochibacoa, at present, there is not enough known to judge if they are *caribes* or *guatraos*, and judgment is reserved until there is sufficient information to be able to say; and from the province of Cochibacoa along the coast it is declared that for present they are to be considered *guatraos* and as friends of the Christians, and this for now resolves any dispute; and in the same way it is declared that the rest of the coast as far as Cochibacoa, except the Unotos, cannot be judged at present for the same reason as mentioned before, that there is not sufficient information; from Cochibacoa as far as the Areu River, which is twenty-five leagues from Darien, because it is not possible to judge if they are *caribes*, or previously *guatraos*, since they are infamous as sodomites, judgment is reserved until there is more information, because, having no other reason to hand, with them there has been no war or conflict; and since the Indians inland, in the above-mentioned region already adjudicated, from Uriapana to the Cabo de Isla Blanco, which is the port of entry for Codera, there are the *guatraos* previously mentioned; but from here their provinces extend into the interior to where there

2. Literally "pottery makers/vendors," this name being consistent with the location of the major archaeological sites of the Barrancoid pottery series on the lower Orinoco River.

3. The northern sea passage between Trinidad and Venezuela.

are those who are judged to be in the condition of *caribes* and are so named and declared as such; and because the island of Trinidad, most notably, is required to be judged by Your Majesty as to its condition, in the light of what has been recorded above, it is especially noted that at present they are to be treated as *guatraos* and friends of the Christians and it is so declared and judged.

As to those provinces and lands mentioned above as those of the *caribes*, it is declared and affirmed that the Christians who travel about those parts with the licenses and instructions they are given are free to enter and take, seize and capture, and make war and hold and possess and trade as slaves those Indians who in the designated islands, lands, and provinces are judged as *caribes*, being permitted to do so in whatever manner, so long as they are first given permission by the justices and officials of Your Majesty; it is also declared that that the *armadas* [war fleets] which are given licenses [shall] take with them *guatraos* of the islands and regions near the *caribes*, in order that they can see that the Christians are not doing harm to the *guatraos*, only to the *caribes*, so that the *guatraos* will agree to come and wish to go along with them willingly; and so in those islands and lands no less than the coast and islands judged by me as *guatraos*, and on the coast named above, this verdict now makes it obligatory, from the highest to the lowest, that among those not judged to be *caribes* it is required and ordered that, as *armadas* or in whatever capacity, they are constrained from making war, violence, extortions, [and] taking by force against their will from these regions, provinces, and islands any persons, livestock, possessions, *guanines* [gold objects], pearls, or any other property: because such wars, use of force and extortion, or theft of food is banned and forbidden by the Majesty of the Queen and Emperor, our lords; but I declare and say that, with proper license and orders given to such *armadas* wishing to go there, it is possible for them voluntarily to investigate and decide if certain Indians are in fact *caribes*; otherwise they are not allowed to take or seize such persons as slaves, [that] being against the prohibitions and authority of Your Majesty over this matter, [and] that no persons will be allowed to go there, nor pass through, under penalty of death and seizure of their possessions, two-thirds of which will be taken by the Royal Treasury and one-third going to the person who denounces or makes the accusation; these penalties will apply to whoever disobeys the said prohibition and authority, no less here on this island of Hispaniola as in other islands or the regions of Tierra Firme or in whatever regions of the Ocean Sea belonging to the monarchs of Castile.

This judgment and sentence is made and recorded in the city of Santo Domingo, being posted in three different public places, and also posted on the islands of Cuba and San Juan [Puerto Rico] so that no one may pretend ignorance of the required letters and licenses from the justices of those islands, which are mandatory; this is done by my sentence, judging, as I have declared and pronounced and given in these writings for them; the said penalties should not be extended to those who use the assistance of the *guatraos* and who trade with willing Indians who are not *caribes*, but are to be used to prevent those Indians being taken as slaves.

Judge Figueroa
Royal Scribe—Diego Cano

Document 5

An Account of the Provinces of the *Aruacas*
by Rodrigo de Navarrete (ca. 1550)

*An account of the provinces and nations that the Indians call **aruacas**, who
inhabit the coast of Tierra-Firme two hundred and more leagues from the island
of Margarita toward where the sun rises. Done at the command of Your Majesty
by me, Rodrigo de Navarrete, inhabitant of the island of Margarita, where the
said Indians come to trade with the Christians, where I took down from them
this account. In order to translate and interpret what the Indians precisely
meant, there was a **morisco** who was among them for twelve years, and others
who have come to understand the language and who are conversant with
their lands*

The provinces of the *aruacas* are above the Amazon River and all
along the coast; the land is low and barely distinguishable from the
sea; they have villages on the banks of the rivers; some of the rivers
that flow through this low country and empty into the sea are very
large and discharge a great volume of water.

The principal river which they inhabit and which they say is the
source of the others is called Bermeji, another is called Curetuy,
another Dumaruni, another Desguixo, another Baorome, and another
Moraca;[1] along the coast from east to west they occupy over three
degrees of latitude. These rivers are full of fish, and on the banks
there is good hunting for tapir, pig, and deer and other varieties of
animals, good hunting for birds, and wide-open plains for livestock
and to grow other foodstuffs.

These Indians are very industrious and are extremely generous.
In winter they devote themselves to work of various kinds, and in

1. Bermeji = Berbice, Curetuy = Corentyn, Dumaruni = Demerara, Desguixo =
Essequibo, Baorome = Pomeroon, and Moraca = Moruca; essentially the coastal region
of modern-day Guyana.

summer[2] they go to war against their enemies the *caribes,* whom they hold in the uttermost enmity, and with whom they consider it the greatest glory to wage war.

The rivers where they are now settled were, they say, formerly under the power of the *caribes,* and according to tradition; as they say, following the memory of their ancestors, they came in ships from where the sun rises, sailed all along that coast, and finding the country very agreeable and fertile, and rich in all kinds of provisions, they settled on the banks of the rivers and made friendship with the *caribes,* who then possessed them. Noticing in the course of time that the *caribes* were bad neighbors and ate other Indians, they were against them, and after long and bloody wars succeeded in driving them out of the rivers and remaining masters of the country, firmly establishing themselves in the place. At this moment the *caribes* hold some of the best and richest lands, and the *aruacas* are trying to take these lands by making war on them; and all this time the *aruacas* carry on this war with even greater care and diligence than the Christians have done in their wars against the Moors, for their hatred is much greater.

At the approach of summer, the *aruacas* build a great many ships, forming an armada of thirty or more pirogues, which are single-masted ships capable of carrying thirty to fifty men. They then set out, sailing along the coast and entering the various rivers in search of the armadas of the *caribes,* who do exactly as the *aruacas.* When they encounter each other, there is a fierce battle. They also raid the villages and all the old people, and carry away the young of both sexes to serve them like slaves as workers; they also sell them to other nations with whom they maintain friendship. As a mark of the slavery of those taken in war, their hair is cut; and this is considered a great disgrace by the *caribes,* who call all such persons *priests.* The *aruacas* say that whenever they find young boys or girls among the captives who are of good disposition and habits, they marry them to their own sons and daughters, and so they turn them into *aruacas:* and in this way they have succeeded in advancing the prosperity of their people and their lands. The *caribes* also treat the *aruacas* whom they capture in battle in a similar fashion, and if the captives are fat and strong they eat them, and if they are thin they stuff them with

---

2. "Winter" and "summer" here refer to the wet and dry seasons in the tropics.

nasty potions, and when they become fat, they eat them; and as a result the *aruacas* hate them intensely and never cease to revenge themselves upon them.

The *aruaca* Indians are of good stature and have noble faces; they curl their hair; their ears are very large and pierced; and they usually put pieces of wood or other things in the holes to make them as large as possible. They are quite naked except that they cover their genitals with a palm leaf. They are extremely friendly with the Christians and make every effort to take them to their country; and, they have taken some and they have been very well treated: if they are asked why they wish the Christians in their lands, they say that because they aid them against the *caribes,* and also because they find there is no nation so good as that of the Christians.

I tried to learn of these *aruaca* Indians what their beliefs were, and also to get some information as to their habits and customs, and for that purpose kept some of them in my own house; for they are accustomed, when visiting this place, to remain among the Christians from one summer to the next. This they do, as they say, for the purpose of learning something from the Christians; and, from those whom I have often have stay in my house, I have understood that their belief and object of adoration is the sky, because they say that in the vast sky there is a great lord and lady, and that this great lord created them and sends them the rain to cause everything to grow on the earth; and the *aruacas* say that it is good to die, for their souls, which they call *Gaguche*,[3] will go up and live with this powerful lord: also that he who is wicked will have his soul taken away when he dies by Camurespitan, which is the name they give to the devil; being asked what it is necessary to be a good *aruaca,* they say they must not kill another *aruaca,* nor deny the things another asks for, and that if anyone comes to their house they will feed them, and that they should not take the belongings or the wife of another *aruaca,* and that they should always be friends and at peace with other *aruacas,* and that the souls of those who do this will go to Hubuiri, as they call the great lord of the sky.[4]

These Indians will not permit any idle people to remain in their country; so that within three days either they work or have to leave

3. Taíno *gua* (great), *goeiz* (spirit).
4. The word *hubuiri* contains the linguistic elements for "high up" and "spirit" in the Lokono language.

their territories; other interesting things I also heard and learned from them, but in order that my account not be doubted, I do not write of this until, in the course of time, they become better known and understood.

These Indians have schools like seminaries, and among them are old and wise men whom they call *cemetu*;[5] and they assemble in houses designed for their meetings, and there these old men recount the traditions and exploits of their ancestors and great men; and also narrate what those ancestors heard from their forefathers; and so they remember ancient things; and, in a similar way they preach about events relating to the sky, to the sun, and to the moon and stars: they are extremely curious; north and all the other markers that the Christians take into account, it seems to me that they know much better, and concerning lightning, comets, and other signs which are in the sky; these things continuously seize them with delight even throughout the night.

These *aruaca* Indians have been more than twenty-five years in commerce and friendship with the Christians of the island of Cubagua, where they land their pirogues, without either being able to interpret the other; they traffic with the Christians, exchanging various handicrafts made from animals and parrots and other birds; they used to call the Christians the *guatraos,* since whenever they saw a Christian they would say *guatrao,* which among them is to say *friend:* in this way, although they have trafficked for a long time with the Christians of these islands, lacking an understanding of their language, they [the Christians] have never learned any of their secrets until, in the year 1545, a *morisco* arrived with them who had been living among them for twelve years: this *morisco* had been carried off from the fleet of Diego de Ordaz, and at the time when this *morisco* came to the island of Margarita I was employed here and interviewed the *morisco,* as well the [native] leaders, who were well treated, with the result that the *morisco* and the Indians remained among the Christians in all safety: and they have come here every summer and, trusting their friendship with the Christians, many bring their wives and children to see the Christians.

During the time I was in command here I took special care that they were well treated; and although some *caciques* have done them

5. Lokono, *semeti* (shaman).

harm because they were looked upon as enemies by some bad Indians and Negroes, and this was used as an excuse for taking the handicrafts they bring on their visits here, now they know how to find justice [through the Spaniards].

All that is contained in this account is taken from conversations with the *morisco* and with a boy of that nation whom I instructed, knew, and understood, as well as other things which I do not mention for the reasons already given: this boy lived with me for two years and in a short time learnt the Ave Maria and Paternoster: and good number of our vassals used to go and come from their territories, and it was very useful means to communicate with their leaders; on occasions there was a great need for provisions in the island, owing to drought, and I sent this boy with a request to the leaders that they provide us with the local bread, and as a result a month later they came with more than two thousand loads of *cacabi*, each load being more than two *arrobas* of *cacabi* bread,[6] and I gave for each load a knife; in this way they have helped us many times, and even today they relieve the hunger in that island, because in their rainy lands the absence of drought means they have no lack of food.

These Indians have many Gypsy habits, especially in being lively, quick-witted, and very friendly toward Christians; also in buying and selling, and in going from place to place, voyaging out from their provinces more than two hundred leagues, or other places along the coast to the east in their ships; and up the rivers of those regions, ascending many and going wherever they wish, and to certain pearl islands where some *caciques*, my friends, would have brought me; and I was all ready with good equipment and provisions, and the sin of envy overwhelmed some Spaniards, so that as I was about to depart on the voyage, their malicious gossip caused me a lot of harm, and those secrets I mentioned remain undisclosed.

Rodrigo de Navarrete,
Royal Scribe—Father Juan Martinez de Santa Cruz

---

6. One *arroba* equals approximately twenty-five pounds of cassava, so 50 tons, or 45.2 tonnes.

REFERENCES

Alegria, Mela Pons. 1980. The Use of Masks, Spectacles, and Eye-pieces Among the Antillean Aborigines. In *Proceedings of the Eighth International Congress for the Study of Pre-Columbian Cultures of the Lesser Antilles,*578–92. Tempe: Arizona State University.

Apter, Andrew. 2002. On African Origins: Creolization and *Connaissance* in Haitian Vodou. *American Ethnologist* 29 (2): 233–60.

Beauvoir-Dominique, Rachel. 1995. Underground Realms of Being: Vodoun Magic. In *Sacred Arts of Haitian Vodou,* edited by Donald Cosentino, 153–77. Los Angeles: Fowler Museum of Cultural History.

Bercht, Fatima, Estrellita Brodsky, John Alan Farmer, and Dicey Taylor, eds. 1997. *Taíno: Pre-Columbian Art and Culture from the Caribbean.* New York: Monacelli Press.

Bourne, Edward Gaylord. 1906. Columbus, Ramon Pane, and the Beginnings of American Anthropology. *Proceedings of the American Antiquarian Society* 17:310–48.

Breton, Raymond. 1665. *Dictionaire Caraibe-François.* Auxerre.

———. 1666. *Dictionaire François-Caraibe.* Auxerre.

Buzard, James. 2003. On Auto-Ethnographic Authority. *Yale Journal of Criticism* 16 (1): 61–91.

Churchill, Awnsham. 1704. *A Collection of Voyages and Travels, Some Now First Printed from Original Manuscripts: Others Translated out of Foreign Languages, and Now First Published in English.* London: A. and J. Churchill.

Columbus, Ferdinand. 1571. *Historie del S. D. Fernando Colombo: Nelle quali s'ha particolare, & vera relatione della vita, & de'fatti dell' Ammiraglio D. Christoforo Colombo, suo padre.* Translated by Alfonso de Ulloa. Venice: Francesco de' Franceschi Sanese.

———. 1992. *The Life of the Admiral Christopher Columbus by His Son Ferdinand.* Rev. ed. Edited by Benjamin Keen. New Brunswick: Rutgers University Press.

Crosby, Alfred W. 1972. *The Columbian Exchange: Biological and Cultural Consequences of 1492.* Westport, Conn.: Greenwood.

Forte, Maximilian C. 2005. *Ruins of Absence, Presence of Caribs: (Post)Colonial Representations of Aboriginality in Trinidad and Tobago.* Gainesville: University Press of Florida.

Frese, Pamela R., and Margaret C. Harrell, eds. 2003. *Anthropology and the United States Military: Coming of Age in the Twenty-first Century.* New York: Palgrave Macmillan.

Gil, Juan, and Consuelo Varela, eds. 1984. *Cartas de particulares a Colón y relaciones coetáneas.* Madrid: Alianza.

Goodman, Alan. 2006. From the President: Engaging with National Security. *Anthropology News* 47 (2): 63.

Guitar, Lynne, ed. 2002. Documenting the Myth of Taíno Extinction. Special issue, *KACIKE: Journal of Caribbean Amerindian History and Anthropology* 3 (1). http://www.kacike.org/GuitarEnglish.pdf.

Harper, Kristin N., Paolo S. Ocampo, Bret M. Steiner, Robert W. George, Michael S. Silverman, Shelly Bolotin, Allan Pillay, Nigel J. Saunders, and George J. Armelegos. 2008. The Origin of the Treponematoses: A Phylogenetic Approach. *Public Library of Science: Neglected Tropical Diseases* 2 (1): 1–13.

Harris, Marvin. 1977. *Cannibals and Kings: The Origins of Cultures.* New York: Random House.

Hulme, Peter, and Neil L. Whitehead, eds. 1992. *Wild Majesty: Encounters with Caribs from Columbus to the Present Day: An Anthology.* Oxford: Oxford University Press.

Keymis, Lawrence. 1596. *A Relation of the Second Voyage to Guiana.* London.

Las Casas, Bartolomé de. 1909. *Apologética historia de las Indias.* Madrid: Bailly, Bailliére é Hijos.

———. 1999. *Brevísima relación de la destruición de las Indias.* Edited by Consuelo Varela. Madrid: Editorial Castalia.

———. 1875–76. *Historia de las Indias.* Edited by Feliciano Ramírez de Arellano Fuensanta del Valle and José León Sancho Rayón. Madrid: Imprenta de Miguel Ginesta.

Lutz, Catherine. 2002. Making War at Home in the United States: Militarization and the Current Crisis. *American Anthropologist* 104 (3): 723–35.

Martyr D'Anghera, Peter. 1530. *De orbe novo decades.* Alcalá de Henares: Michaele de Eguia.

———. 1912. *De Orbo Novo: The Eight Decades of Peter Martyr D'Anghera.* Edited by Francis A. MacNutt. London: Macmillan.

Montaigne, Michel de. 2007. *Les Essais.* Paris: Gallimard.

Ojer, Pablo. 1966. *La formación del oriente venezolano.* Caracas: Universidad Católica "Andrés Bello," Facultad de Humanidades y Educación, Instituto de Investigaciones Históricas.

Oliver, José. R. 2009. *Caciques and Cemi Idols: The Web Spun by Taíno Rulers Between Hispaniola and Puerto Rico.* Tuscaloosa: University of Alabama Press.

Otte, Enrique. 1977. *Las Perlas del Caribe.* Caracas: Fundación John Boulton.

Pagden, Anthony. 1982. *The Fall of Natural Man: The American Indian and the Origins of Comparative Ethnology.* Cambridge Iberian and Latin American Studies. Cambridge: Cambridge University Press.

Pané, Ramón. 1988. *Relación Acerca de Las Antigüedades de Los Indios*. 8th ed. Edited by José Juan Arrom. Coyocán: Siglo Veintiuno. First edition 1974.

———. 1999. *An Account of the Antiquities of the Indians*. Edited by José Juan Arrom. Translated by Susan C. Griswold. Durham: Duke University Press.

Perkins, Constance G. Janiga. 2007. *Reading, Writing, and Translation in the "Relación acerca de las antigüedades de los indios" (c. 1498) by Fray Ramón Pané: A Study of a Pioneering Work in Ethnography*. Lewiston, N.Y.: Edwin Mellen Press.

Pinkerton, John, ed. 1814. *A General Collection of the Best and Most Interesting Voyages and Travels in All Parts of the World*. London: Longman, Hurst, Rees and Orme.

Price, David. 2008. *Anthropological Intelligence: The Deployment and Neglect of American Anthropology in the Second World War*. Durham: Duke University Press.

Rafinesque, C. S. 1836. *A life of travels and researches in North America and South Europe; or, outlines of the life, travels and researches of C. S. Rafinesque . . . containing his travels in North America and the south of Europe; the Atlantic Ocean, Mediterranean, Sicily, Azores, &c., from 1802 to 1835—with sketches of his scientific and historical researches &c*. Philadelphia: Printed for the author by F. Turner.

Ralegh, Walter. 1997. *The Discoverie of the Large, Rich and Bewtiful Empyre of Guiana*. Edited by Neil L. Whitehead. Exploring Travel Series 1; American Exploration and Travel Series 71. Manchester: Manchester University Press; Norman: University of Oklahoma Press.

Restall, Matthew, ed. 2005. *Beyond Black and Red: African-Native Relations in Colonial Latin America*. Albuquerque: University of New Mexico Press.

Robben, Antonius C. G. M. 2005. Anthropology at War? What Argentina's Dirty War Can Teach Us. *Anthropology News* 46 (6): 5.

Rouse, Irving. 1948. The West Indies. In *Handbook of South American Indians*, edited by Julian Haynes Steward, vol. 4, *The Circum-Caribbean Tribes*, 495–566. Washington, D.C: Smithsonian Institution, Bureau of American Ethnology.

Salomon, Frank, and Stuart B. Schwartz, eds. 1999. *South America*. Vol. 3 of *The Cambridge History of the Native Peoples of the Americas*. Cambridge: Cambridge University Press.

Santos-Granero, Fernando. 2009. *The Occult Life of Things: Native Amazonian Theories of Materiality and Personhood*. Tucson: University of Arizona Press.

Sauer, Carl Ortwin. 2008. *The Early Spanish Main*. Cambridge: Cambridge University Press.

Southey, Robert. 1819. *History of Brazil*. London: Longman, Hurst, Rees.

Stevens-Arroyo, Antonio M. 1988. *Cave of the Jagua: The Mythological World of the Taínos*. Albuquerque: University of New Mexico Press.

Steverlynck, Astrid. 2008. Amerindian Amazons: Women, Exchange, and the Origins of Society. *Journal of the Royal Anthropological Institute* 14 (3): 572–89.

Sued Badillo, Jalil. 1978. *Los Caribes: Realidad o fabulá*. Rio Piedras: Editorial Antillana.

———. 1995. New Approaches to the Question of Ethnicity in the Early Colonial Caribbean. In *Wolves from the Sea: Readings in the Archaeology and Anthropology of the Island Carib*, edited by Neil L. Whitehead, 61–90. Leiden: KITLV Press.

———. 2003. *Autochthonous Societies*. General History of the Caribbean 1. London: Macmillan Caribbean.

Taylor, Douglas MacRae. 1977. *Languages of the West Indies*. Johns Hopkins Studies in Atlantic History and Culture. Baltimore: Johns Hopkins University Press.

Varela, Consuelo, and Isabel Aguirre. 2006. *La caída de Cristóbal Colon: El juicio de Bobadilla*. Madrid: Marcial Pons Historia.

Wakin, Eric. 1994. Anthropology Goes to War: Professional Ethics and Counterinsurgency in Thailand. *American Ethnologist* 21 (4): 996–97.

Warner, Marina. 2002. *Fantastic Metamorphoses, Other Worlds: Ways of Telling the Self*. Oxford: Oxford University Press.

Whitehead, Neil L. 1988. *Lords of the Tiger Spirit: A History of the Caribs in Colonial Venezuela and Guyana, 1498–1920*. Dordrecht: Foris.

———. 1990. Carib Ethnic Soldiering in Venezuela, the Guianas, and the Antilles, 1492–1820. *Ethnohistory* 37 (4): 357–85.

———, ed. 1995. *Wolves from the Sea: Readings in the Anthropology of the Island Carib*. Leiden: KITLV Press.

———. 1996. The Mazaruni Dragon: Golden Metals and Elite Exchanges in the Caribbean, Orinoco, and the Amazon. In *Chieftains, Power, and Trade: Regional Interaction in the Intermediate Area of the Americas*, edited by Carl H. Langebaek and F. Cárdenas-Arroyo, 107–32. Bogotá: Departamento de Antropología, Universidad de los Andes.

———. 1999a. The Crises and Transformations of Invaded Societies: The Caribbean (1492–1580). In Salomon and Schwartz 1999, pt. 1, 864–903.

———. 1999b. Lowland Peoples Confront Colonial Regimes in Northern South America, 1550–1900. In Salomon and Schwartz 1999, pt. 2, 382–441.

———. 2002a. Arawak Linguistic and Cultural Identity Through Time: Contact, Colonialism, and Creolization. In *Comparative Arawakan Histories*, edited by Jonathan D. Hill and Fernando Santos-Granero, 51–73. Urbana: University of Illinois Press.

———. 2002b. *Dark Shamans: Kanaimà and the Poetics of Violent Death*. Durham: Duke University Press.

———. 2009. Ethnography, Torture, and the Human Terrain / Terror Systems. *Fast Capitalism* 5(2). http://fastcapitalism.com.

Whitehead, Neil L., and Stephanie W. Alemán, eds. 2009. *Anthropologies of Guayana: Cultural Spaces in Northeastern Amazonia.* Tucson: University of Arizona Press.

Whitehead, Neil L., and Robin Wright, eds. 2004. *In Darkness and Secrecy: The Anthropology of Assault Sorcery and Witchcraft in Amazonia.* Durham: Duke University Press.

Wilbert, Johannes. 1987. *Tobacco and Shamanism in South America.* New Haven: Yale University Press.

Wilson, Samuel. 1990. *Hispaniola: Caribbean Chiefdoms in the Age of Columbus.* Tuscaloosa: University of Alabama Press.

Archives

AGI: Archivo General de Indias, Seville.

CDI: Colleción de Documentos Inéditos, Madrid, 1864–84.

latin american originals

Series Editor | Matthew Restall

This series features primary source texts on colonial and nineteenth-century Latin America, translated into English, in slim, accessible, affordable editions that also make scholarly contributions. Most of these sources are being published in English for the first time, and represent an alternative to the traditional texts on early Latin America. The initial focus is on the conquest period in sixteenth-century Spanish America, but subsequent volumes include Brazil, as well as later centuries. The series features archival documents and printed sources originally in Spanish, Portuguese, Latin, and various Native American languages. The contributing authors are historians, anthropologists, art historians, and scholars of literature.

Matthew Restall is Edwin Erle Sparks Professor of Latin American History and Anthropology, and Director of Latin American Studies, at the Pennsylvania State University. He is co-editor of *Ethnohistory* journal. J. Michael Francis is Professor of Latin American History at the University of North Florida.

Associate Series Editor | J. Michael Francis

Board of Editorial Consultants
Noble David Cook | Edward F. Fischer | Susan Kellogg
Elizabeth W. Kiddy | Kris E. Lane | Alida C. Metcalf
Susan Schroeder | John F. Schwaller | Ben Vinson III

Titles in print